EAT MALAYSIA & SINGAPORE

The complete companion to Malaysia & Singapore's cuisine and food culture

CONTENTS

INTRODUCTION

There's no question about it. Malaysians and Singaporeans are food-obsessed – no sooner have they finished one meal than they are thinking about the next. The mix of ethnicities and multicultural traditions in these neighbouring, historically linked countries offer the food lover a gastronomic experience like no other.

Variety is the spice of life. In Malaysia and Singapore, that claim certainly rings true. Here a simple staple like rice is transformed from *bubur* (rice porridge) to *nasi lemak* (coconut rice), from *ketupat* (compressed rice) to *tuak* (rice wine). Fancy noodles? Take your pick from a mesmerising selection – some made from rice flour, some from wheat flour and others from mung beans – served up in flavoursome soups or as a foil for the sizzling contents of a wok.

With opportunities to eat or drink around every corner, you'll never go hungry or thirsty in Malaysia and Singapore. Sure, there are fine dining and Michelin-starred restaurants here, but more often the tastiest food is served in the humblest of surroundings and involves the least amount of fuss. Seemingly countless vendors serve mouth-watering dishes from mobile carts, hawker stalls and shophouses, many employing recipes and techniques handed down from previous generations. The food is delicious and hygiene standards are high, so you should have no fear of eating wherever and whenever you like.

Every dish offers fresh insight to the history and culture of this colourful region. Centuries of trade, colonisation and immigration have left their mark on Malaysia and Singapore in the form of cuisines so multifaceted it would take months of nonstop grazing to truly grasp their breadth. Nowhere else in Asia are the elements of three great culinary traditions – those of China, India and the Malay Archipelago – so intertwined. A mouthful of *babi pong teh* (stewed pork) reveals, for example, how Malay cooking techniques and Chinese ingredients have found their way into a unique marriage of two cultures. In any local curry you can recognise complex spice accents – turmeric, cumin, coriander – the culinary legacy of the Arab and Indian merchants who tarried upon the shores of the Malay Peninsula and its surrounding islands. For every delightfully multicultural dish there are starkly monocultural ones to enjoy, too. In Malaysia and Singapore you are seldom far from cooks who specialise in making authentic regional Chinese dishes and others who specialise in *dosa*, the crispy-edged crêpes made of rice and lentil flour that are a staple of southern Indian cuisine.

For a visitor it's all so easily accessible thanks to restaurant signs and menus that are in English, and the fact that most vendors speak English alongside Malay and a Chinese or Indian language. What unites everyone is their overwhelming passion for food and their willingness to share this – you will likely find yourself smothered in culinary companionship! The traveller who makes the effort to partake of the region's edible delights will undoubtedly make a few *makan kari* (food friends) along the way. Simply put, in these countries it's not 'How are you?' but '*Sundah makan*?' (Have you eaten yet?).

HISTORY & CULTURE

The food cultures of Malaysia and Singapore have developed out of these neighbouring countries being home, in centuries past, to key trading ports along the Spice Route from Asia to Europe. Any attempt to speak of an overarching Malaysian or Singaporean cuisine is laughable – just as it's near impossible to pick out the average Malaysian or Singaporean person based on a list of physical traits. Yes, some classic dishes such as *nasi lemak* (coconut rice) and chilli crab (mud crab stir-fried in a spicy chilli and tomato-based sauce) have become so closely associated with their home countries that it is possible to identify them as being quintessentially Malaysian or Singaporean. However, what and how locals eat in their daily lives is so diverse and ever-changing that it is only appropriate to speak of the cuisines, rather than the cuisine, of Malaysia and Singapore. The food of the region is as varied as its people and thrives on a complex fusion afforded by a long history of trade and migration.

ORIGIN STORY

It is important to bear in mind that Malaysia and Singapore, as we know them today, emerged as separate independent countries only in the early 1960s. Prior to that, the states of Peninsular Malaysia, Malaysian Borneo and the island of Singapore were loosely amalgamated as a British colony. Between the early 16th century and the early 19th century there were also episodes of Portuguese and Dutch colonisation. And before that, the region was comprised of fragmented, independent Malay kingdoms with disparate allegiances.

Beyond the impact of geographical proximity and a shared history, culinary developments within each state seem have been influenced far more by the political and cultural traditions of neighbouring countries. For example, the Malaysian states close to the Thai border have assimilated their northern neighbours' penchant for sour and spicy flavours. In Melaka, Kristang cuisine is a combination of Portuguese cooking methods and Malay ingredients. Islam, which began to be adopted across the peninsula in the 15th century, has also had profound influence on what people eat and drink here.

6

Today, while the states of the peninsula, together with Sabah and Sarawak on Borneo, form Malaysia, the food of Malaysia is by no means homogeneous across the territory. Some regions along the west coast, where Chinese and Indians have settled, exhibit different cuisine styles from the predominantly Malay and Muslim states of the east coast. Laksa (a spicy, soupy noodle dish) served in Penang tastes nothing like its namesake in Singapore; ask for a chicken curry recipe and you're likely to be asked if you want the Indian, Malay or Chinese version of the dish.

Left: A farmer harvesting rice

Above: Buffalo are traditionally used to plough rice fields

THE MELAKA EMPIRE

Many historians consider the growth of Melaka, on the west coast of Peninsular Malaysia, into a major port sometime around 1400 to be the identifiable starting point for the region's multicultural (and multiculinary) history. Parameswara, a renegade Hindu prince or pirate (take your pick) from a little kingdom in southern Sumatra, washed up around 1401 in the tiny fishing village that would become Melaka. As a seafarer, Parameswara recognised a good port when he saw it and he immediately lobbied the Ming emperor of China for protection from the Thais in exchange for generous trade deals. Thus, the Chinese first came to the Malay Peninsula.

Merchants, traders and missionaries with their own idiosyncratic gastronomic preferences were drawn to Melaka's shores. The port's pattern of government and lifestyle became the basis of what was later termed 'traditional' Malay culture and statecraft. But it would be erroneous to suppose that it was only then that the region established itself as a cultural and culinary crossroads. Even the Orang Asli, the indigenous peoples

8

of the Malay Peninsula, are said to have moved down the peninsula some 10,000 years ago, from the region in western China (roughly, the region called Qinghai Province today) where the great rivers of east and Southeast Asia originate.

RICE CULTIVATION & ANIMAL DOMESTICATION

Some historians argue that the proto-Malays, ancestors of today's Malays, were part of a later wave of immigrants who were ethnically similar to the people of Indonesia. They still share some cooking techniques and preferences for certain spices and flavours. The proto-Malays first settled in the coastal regions and then moved inland, marrying Orang Asli, the peninsula's indigenous tribal people, and blurring the divisions between the two groups in the process. They brought with them knowledge of irrigated rice-field cultivation and the domestication of the ox and buffalo – the beginnings of agriculture. Yet, knowledge of the early history of the region, particularly its culinary history, is at best still hazy. This makes it difficult to identify the specifics of its development.

By the end of the Middle Ages, when the Portuguese arrived, the Malay Archipelago had for

MALAY, MALAYS & MALAYSIAN

Let's get this right. Malay, or more specifically Bahasa Malaysia, is the national language of Malaysia. The Malays are the indigenous people of Malaysia, and form one of the four main races in Singapore. Their traditions and way of life are described as Malay culture. Malaysians, on the other hand, are citizens of Malaysia. This means that an individual may be Chinese and Malaysian, or Indian and Malaysian.

hundreds of years been part of a complex trading network stretching from Africa to China. The northeast monsoon brought Chinese junks laden with silks, brocades, porcelain, pickles and other foodstuffs; Arab and Indian traders sailed in with the southwest monsoon bearing – among their precious metals, ebony and perfumes – fennel and spices such as cardamom and peppercorns. Southeast Asia was already, by then, divided into two main cultural areas: one where Indian influence predominated, and the other (consisting of Tongking, Annam and Cochin China) where Chinese influence stood strong. Gastronomically and culturally the fusion had already begun.

Above: Stone Buddha, Chin Swee Caves Temple, Genting Highlands

THE RELIGIOUS IMPACT

The traders also brought their religious beliefs, along with specific dietary philosophies and habits. The growth of trade with India (particularly South India) brought the coastal peoples of the Malay world into contact with two major religions, Hinduism and Buddhism. From the late 7th century until its demise hundreds of years later (when Melaka rose to take its place), the great Sumatran-based Srivijaya Empire, with its capital in Palembang (Indonesia), is said to have played a significant role in disseminating Hindu-Buddhist ideas in the region. More importantly, its language of government and court has also been described as an early version of the Malay spoken in Melaka, the focal point from which much of the Malay world view and society developed, unchallenged, until the 19th century.

Melaka, in turn, contributed to the evolution of Malay culture by incorporating Islamic ideas into its foundations (Indian Muslim traders are said to have been an impetus for Islam's appearance in Southeast Asia) and encouraging the widespread use of the Malay language in the archipelago simply through its trading power and highly cosmopolitan society. The evolution of Malay cuisine, as such, is influenced by the tenets of Islam, which prohibits the consumption of pork and alcohol.

However, the region's culinary melting pot only truly started to bubble with the arrival of the Portuguese (1511), Dutch (1641) and British (1786), in addition to the Minangkabau from Sumatra (Indonesia) in the 17th century. British rule also radically altered the ethnic composition of the region as Chinese and Indian migrants were brought into the country to work in its mines, tap its rubber trees, build its railways and staff the colonial civil service and police force.

MALAY CUISINE

Malay food is the result of centuries of foreign interaction – from Thai and Indonesian neighbours to Chinese and Indian migrants.

Malay culture arguably crystallised around Melaka's rise as a regional seaport and Islamic centre from the 15th century onwards. The people of the Malay Peninsula's west coast developed a culinary style greatly influenced by visiting (and later settling) traders from Indonesia, India, the Middle East and China. Many of the spices and ingredients central to Malay cooking were first introduced by Indians and Arabs – including pepper, cloves and cardamom.

Basic cooking techniques involve preparing one wet and one dry set of ingredients needed to flavour the dish. Key wet ingredients include shallots, ginger, garlic, fresh chillies and fresh turmeric and are traditionally blended using a *batu lesong* (mortar and pestle), although modern cooks sometimes choose to use a kitchen blender. The technique is to first combine the wet ingredients and then fry them in oil before adding dry ingredients such as toasted then ground coriander seed, cumin, aniseed, cloves, cinnamon and cardamom. Indian cooking uses the same technique.

Rice is always the foundation of a Malay meal, and Malaysia produces its own rice. It may be steamed, boiled or fried, cooked on its own or flavoured with coconut milk, spices and herbs. It can be *ketupat* (steamed in angular little pockets woven out of coconut fronds) or *lemang* (cooked over a charcoal fire in bamboo poles lined with young banana leaves). Whichever rice is served, it is customary to have it with a fish (or seafood) curry, a meat or poultry dish (or both), two or more vegetable dishes and a selection of *sambals* (chilli-based condiments). Indonesian-influenced dry curries like beef *rendang* (beef in a thick coconut-milk curry sauce) have become a permanent feature at *nasi lemak* stalls, while more recently, Chinese dishes such as *bee hoon* (rice vermicelli) and *cheng teng* (a syrupy dessert filled with nuts and dried fruit) are not uncommon on the menus at Malay weddings.

Islam was introduced to the region by Indian Muslim merchants from Gujarat and Malays have, over the years, absorbed a tradition of Middle Eastern dishes interpreted with Indian overtones. Dishes include *nasi biryani* (rice casserole often layered with meat and steamed gently so that the flavours blend) and chicken *korma* (rich, thickened, mild curry). In recent times, Malay homemakers are as likely to buy ready-mixed curry paste from the South Indian vendor at their neighbourhood wet market for a fish curry as they are to use the Indian curry leaf for seasoning. Malay cooks will also whip up *roti canai* (flaky fried flat bread), which Indians enjoy with curry; Malays, however, prefer to sprinkle it with sugar and eat it as a snack.

WHAT'S HALAL?

Muslim dietary laws forbid alcohol, pork and all pork-based products. Restaurants where it's ok for Muslims to dine will be clearly labelled halal; this is a stricter definition than places that label themselves simply 'pork free'. For meat to be considered halal, or permitted, the animal's jugular vein has to be severed while the butcher recites the name of Allah, as prescribed in the Quran (the Muslim holy book).

Left: The wild red jungle fowl is an ancestor of the domestic chicken

ORANG ASLI CUISINE

There are still communities of Orang Alsi people living in Malaysia today, who continue to keep to their nomadic lifestyles, relying on traditional crops and hunting. They are the oldest indigenous inhabitants of Peninsular Malaysia (their name means 'original people'), but it's unlikely that you'll get to sample their cuisine. Accounting for just 0.6% of the national population, Orang Asli are nearly all rural- and jungle-dwelling and are divided into dozens of scattered tribes, each with their own language and cultural practices. As they are marginalised from mainstream society, the foods of the Orang Asli have generally not entered the Malaysian and Singaporean food lexicon.

Orang Asli foods and cooking tend to be very simple and dependent on what grows or lives in the forest around them. These include different varieties of ferns, green shoots, turmeric, pandan leaves and lemongrass. Aromatic leaves like *daun semomok* and *kulim* that provide onion- and garlic-type flavours, and *bunga kantan* (torch ginger), which is common in Malay and Peranakan cooking, can also be used. If there is a staple food it is tapioca, but some tribes do also grow their own heirloom varieties of rice. Protein sources might include jungle fowl, wild boar, freshwater fish and, for tribes living along coastlines, saltwater fish. Foods also tend to be boiled or roasted over fire rather than fried in oil.

DAYAK CUISINE

Malaysian Borneo's indigenous peoples, known collectively as Dayaks, belong to more than 50 different ethnic groups that speak about 140 languages and dialects. Borneo's indigenous peoples are remarkably diverse, expressing themselves with a rich variety of languages, traditions and artistic forms. But when it comes to cooking, they all turn to pretty much the same uniquely Bornean selection of leaves, flowers, fruits, roots, vines, ferns, fish and meats that the rainforest shares with all who know its edible secrets.

Each indigenous tribe has its own ideas about the best way to combine, season and prepare the natural bounty of the forest. Some dishes are tangy, others bitter or surprisingly spicy, and yet others characterised by peaty, jungly flavours unknown in other Asian culinary traditions. Many dishes are cooked and/or served in leaves (such as *daun isip*, used by the Kelabits) that add delicate flavours in addition to serving as ecofriendly packaging and plates. Parcels of glutinous rice wrapped in a leaf – sometimes with meat, too – is a typical 'packed lunch' to bring with you when hiking from longhouse to longhouse in the highlands. Some ingredients, such

as ferns, are so perishable they have to be eaten within a day of being picked, so exporting them – even to Peninsular Malaysia – is virtually impossible. As a result the only way to experience the mouth-watering, eye-opening and tongue-tickling world of Dayak cuisine is to come to Borneo.

But even on the island, sampling Dayak cuisine – naturally organic and MSG-free – is rarely as easy as walking up to a hawker centre. There are a handful of restaurants in cities such as Kuching, Miri and Kota Kinabalu – of special note is The Dyak, a pioneering gourmet establishment in Kuching – but otherwise the only way to savour indigenous dishes is to dine at a longhouse or be invited to dinner in a family home.

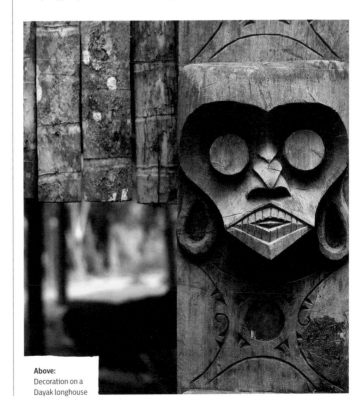

Above:
Decoration on a
Dayak longhouse

CHINESE CUISINE

The key elements of Chinese cuisine are the freshness of ingredients and a careful balance between tastes, textures and temperatures: sweet and sour, hot and cold, plain and spicy.

Chinese culture has had a strong influence on the region since at least the 15th century. But it was only in the early 19th century, drawn by the profitability of tin mining and plantation agriculture, that the Chinese population in the region grew dramatically. By 1827, the Chinese were the largest single community in Singapore, and by 1845 they formed more than half its population. Most came from China's southeast provinces of Guangdong, Fujian and Guangxi and belonged to five major sociolinguistic groups: Teochew, Cantonese, Hokkien, Hakka and Hainanese. The Chinese community of Penang, which forms over 40% of the state's population, also has a similar ethnic background.

Each of these migrants brought with them their regional cuisines. Rice forms the basis of their meals and it is usually served with an assortment of meat, seafood, poultry and vegetable dishes. It's often said that Chinese will eat almost anything that is alive; at formal dining occasions, the validity of that claim is constantly reaffirmed. Birds-nest soup (made from the edible nests of swiflets), *hai shen* (braised sea cucumber; sea slug) and *ya jiao* (duck feet) are just some of the dishes that are considered delicacies among Chinese. But more often than not, the meals most Chinese have at home are simple: a clear soup, a stir-fried vegetable dish and a fish or meat dish accompanied with steamed rice.

To Chinese, 'meat' is near synonymous with pork, although with growing contemporary health consciousness, chicken and fish are quickly overtaking pork as the protein of choice. Lamb was not popular until quite recently, while beef is avoided by practising Chinese Buddhists – in fact, the strictest Buddhist adherents enjoy a vegetarian diet.

While they continue to eat pretty much the same food as their ancestors, Chinese in the Malaysian and Singaporean region have also modified their food in ways that reveal the long interaction they've had with other racial groups. Chinese 'cookboys' (the Hainanese have been long associated with this profession) who worked for colonial employers learnt to reproduce English food and incorporated some of the techniques and flavourings into their own food. For example, they quickly realised the potential of tomato sauce, Worcestershire auce and spiced fruit-based condiments like HP Sauce, which they then used to flavour Chinese-style pork chops (now a favourite in its own right) and fried fish, and turned into a dip for *inche kabin* (spicy fried chicken pieces).

Below: Chinese steamed buns in Kuala Lumpur's Chinatown

REGIONAL CHINESE CUISINES

Cantonese is the most common of the regional Chinese cuisines you'll find in Malaysia and Singapore, with typical dishes including *xiao long bao* (dumplings filled with hot soup) and dim sum (also known as yum cha), snack-type dishes usually eaten at breakfast and lunchtime or as a Sunday brunch in large, noisy restaurants.

Many of Singapore's Chinese are Hokkien, whose hearty noodle dishes include *char kway teow* (stir-fried noodles with cockles, Chinese sausage and dark sauces), *bak chor mee* (noodles with pork, meat balls and fried scallops) and *Hokkien mee* (yellow egg noodles with prawns, served either fried or in a rich prawn-based stock).

Seafood is a speciality of delicate Teochew cuisine, with fish maw (a fish's swim bladder) cropping up alarmingly often. The classic Teochew comfort food is *congee* – rice porridge, served with fish, pork and even frogs' legs.

A TOUCH OF SPICE

Life alongside chilli-loving Malays and Indians also inspired the Chinese to appreciate a touch of spiciness in their food. Hawker favourites such as *wonton mee* (*wonton* noodles; fine, yellow noodles served with minced pork dumplings), *char kway teow* and Hainanese chicken rice are now served with a side dish of chilli – either pickled, chopped and topped with light soy sauce or blended and served with minced ginger. Chilli has become just as important as the chicken and the rice when a diner assesses the quality of a Hainanese chicken-rice dish. Malay-style curries are also served in Chinese homes.

CHICKEN RICE

Hainanese chicken rice is Singapore's de facto national dish. Slices of steamed fowl are served atop flavoursome rice cooked in chicken stock, with slices of cucumber and ginger, chilli and soy dips.

INDIAN CUISINE

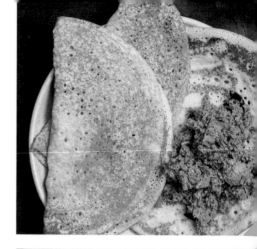

Much of Malaysia and Singapore's delicious Indian cuisine is South Indian in character and taste because that's where the region's Indian population originally hailed from.

While the region was influenced by Indian culture long before Europeans appeared on the scene, Indians only really made their presence felt in the 19th century when migration from the subcontinent to British Malaya was ramped up during colonial rule. Most of the Indian population are Hindus with their ancestral roots from South India and Sri Lanka; in particular, you'll encounter many people of Tamil descent.

In southern India the staple food is rice, usually eaten with *daal* (cooked pulses), vegetables and pickles, although fish or meat may be added. Dishes tend to be searingly spicy because it is believed that in warm climates, chilli cools the body through perspiration. Coconut milk and yogurt play commanding roles, and mustard seeds are widely used as a spice. Hindus do not eat beef, and some orthodox Hindus feel that frequently used cutlery is unhygienic, preferring to eat with the fingers of the right hand.

18

From top: *Dosa* with coconut *sambal*; Offerings for Thaipusam festival; Sri Mariamman Temple, Singapore

BANANA—LEAF MEALS

Many Hindus are strictly vegetarian and across Malaysia and Singapore, the term 'banana-leaf rice', or simply 'banana leaf', is used to describe a popular Indian meal, which is essentially a *thali* – a one-plate meal made up of several different dishes. Originally from South India, banana leaf consists of a mound of plain rice, with three or four different vegetable dishes served on a banana leaf cut to fit the glorious spread. It is also quite common to have banana-leaf meals with meat or fish components.

The banana-leaf meal can be enhanced with chutneys, pickles as well as a runny meat or fish curry (more like a thick gravy) poured over the white rice. Vegetarians can opt for spinach or onion curries as well as chickpea- or lentil-based *daal*. No banana-leaf meal would be complete without crunchy *pappadam* – large crisps made out of lentil, chickpea and gram flour as well as rice flour. It's also common for a sour soup called *rasam* to be served, alongside an option of plain yogurt.

The refreshing yogurt drink *lassi*, which can be ordered salty or sweet and sometimes flavoured with fruits such as mango and banana, is ideal drink to counter the fiery banana-leaf curries.

NORTH INDIAN CUISINE

For Malaysian and Singaporean Indians of North Indian descent, the staple food is wheat, in various forms of *roti* (various types of bread). North Indian dishes tend to contain more meat and are less fiery than those from South India. Familiar items include *tandoori* (spice-marinated meat cooked in a *tandoor* – a clay oven) dishes served with *naan* (bread made from plain flour and cooked in a *tandoor*). Cow's milk, cream and *ghee* (clarified butter), rather than coconut milk, tend to form the basis of curries.

MAMAK INDIAN CUISINE

Mamak or Indian Muslim hawker dishes (where no pork is used) are in a special class of their own. *Mamak* dishes are quick, one-dish meals eaten by Muslims and non-Muslims alike, that feature a fusion of regional ingredients and flavours. Hot favourites include *mee rebus* (thick, fresh egg noodles in a viscous, sweet and spicy sauce, served with hard-boiled eggs and freshly cut green chillies); *mee goreng* (a spicy fried noodle dish); the pan-fried bread *murtabak* filled with either vegetable or meat stuffings; and the *mamak* version of *rojak* (a salad including deep-fried vegetables and seafood served with spicy-sweet sauce and fresh cucumber, tomato and onion).

PERANAKAN CUISINE

Also known as Nonya cuisine, Peranakan food fuses Malay ingredients with Chinese cooking techniques, reflecting the culturally entwined roots of the Peranakan communities across Singapore and in parts of Malaysia.

Peranakan loosely translates as 'mixed race' in Malay, an apt reflection of their heritage: Peranakans are descendants of Chinese immigrants who, from the 16th century onwards, settled principally in Singapore, Melaka and Penang and married Malay women. History also has it that a Chinese emperor dispatched one of his princesses to Sultan Iskandar Shah of Melaka together with a retinue of 500 handmaidens. The children of these 'gift brides' for the local menfolk eventually came to form the first Peranakan community.

The culture and language of the Peranakans is a fascinating melange of Chinese and Malay traditions. The Peranakans took the name and religion of their Chinese fathers, but the customs, language and dress of their Malay mothers. They also used the terms Straits-born or Straits Chinese to distinguish themselves from later arrivals from China. Another name you may hear for these people is Baba-Nonyas,

after the Peranakan words for men *(baba)* and women *(nonya*, also sometimes spelled *nyonya*).

The Peranakans were often wealthy traders who could afford to indulge their passions for the finer things in life, including food. Because women were predominantly the cooks, the food is also commonly known as Nonya cuisine. The recipes reflect the cultural mix of the community – Malay ingredients and spices such as *belacan* (fermented shrimp paste), chilli, lemongrass, galangal and fresh turmeric are fused with Chinese cooking techniques (including a penchant for pork) and elements of Indian, Thai and Portuguese Eurasian cuisines.

Dishes are often labour-intensive to prepare, but the ensuing gossip and social interaction is an essential part of the whole kitchen experience. One such dish is *ayam buah keluak*, a sour, midly spicy chicken dish flavoured with tamarind and *buah keluak*

BATU LESONG – A NONYA'S METTLE

A Nonya (Straits-born Chinese) lady was trained from an early age in all the domestic arts – cooking, sewing and a demure subservient manner being the quintessential qualities sought-after in a good Peranakan daughter-in-law. Such importance was placed on a girl's prowess in the kitchen that matchmakers often called in at inopportune hours – before mealtimes, when the kitchen was bustling with food preparations and when the *rempah* (spice paste) was being pounded. This was to investigate if the prospective bride fulfilled the key criteria – it was said that matchmakers could detect by the sound of the *batu lesong* (mortar and pestle) which ingredient was being pounded and whether the person who was pounding was an experienced cook. A rhythmic pattern to the pounding gave away a good cook's presence. Mastering the art of the *batu lesong* was a Nonya's rite of passage – the pounding of an assortment of spices to just the right degree of pastiness: smooth yet not liquid, textured yet not coarse.

(also known as *pangium edule*), the large seeds of the kepayang tree. The kernels naturally contain hydrogen cyanide and can be lethal. Before being sold the seeds are boiled, buried in sand (which is then burned) and left to ferment for 40 days. This turns them a pale shade of grey and imparts a smoked, earthy flavour. Before cooking, to completely remove the ash and to leech out any remaining poison, the nuts must be soaked for at least 48 hours with several changes of water. Once cooked, the flesh of the dark-brown nut is rich and creamy, a bit like truffles or black garlic.

Other classic Peranakan dishes include *otak otak* (mildly spicy fish paste wrapped in banana leaves), various types of *kuih* (or *kueh*, sweets and cakes), the Thai-influenced *mee siam* (a spicy, tangy noodle dish) and *babi pong teh* (stewed pork). Peranakan food is usually served with plain rice and eaten communally, as with Chinese food.

TOP HATS

A classic Peranakan finger food is kuih pie tee. *It's also known as 'top hats' because of the shape of the crispy pastry shell filled with julienned jicama (a type of yam), carrot and chopped shrimp.*

(

Left: St Paul's Church, Melaka
Below: British-influenced Eurasian breakfast

EURASIAN CUISINE

This hybrid style of cooking sees European ingredients such as vinegar and Worcestershire sauce used in Asian dishes, and European dishes adapted to Asian ingredients and tastes.

Eurasians have a complex East–West heritage, the result of years of intermarriages between the native people of Malaysia and Singapore with European traders and colonisers. Their dishes blend exotic ingredients drawn from a variety of cultural backgrounds – a dash of Portuguese, Dutch and British together with Indian, Chinese and Malay, mixed liberally with other European and Asian traditions.

In Melaka, the descendants of 16th-century Portuguese traders, explorers and eventually colonisers call themselves Jenti Kristang (Christian people) and speak their own language, a Creole Portuguese that is now often coloured with English, Malay and Chinese phrases. The early Portuguese established a policy of racial integration that sanctioned marriage between themselves and the local people. Intent on incorporating Melaka's native cuisine into their own, they combined ingredients of the local cuisines (which were a hybrid of Malay, Chinese, Indian, Arab and Peranakan cultures) with Portuguese cooking methods.

Today, they use tamarind, lemongrass, lime and galangal to create exotic curries, *sambals*, soups and vegetable dishes – occasionally using alcohol to add a touch of variety to meat and fish dishes. From the Peranakans they acquired a taste for sweet-and-sour dishes along with the art of chopping vegetables, which they stir-fry the Chinese way. Signature dishes include *curry debal* (devil curry, served at Christmas and incorporating ingredients such as ham, luncheon meat or sausages) and *feng* (a pork curry and Christmas speciality that is best eaten a day old).

British colonial culinary influence comes in the form of local versions of chicken pie, corned beef cutlets, oxtail soup and shepherd's pie (minced meat flavoured here with soy and oyster sauce and topped with mashed potato).

A standard formal Eurasian dinner consists of seven to eight dishes: two curries, a fried or roasted dish, a pie, cooked vegetables and a salad, pickles and *sambals*, and a variety of cakes for dessert. Savoury dishes are placed on the table at the same time and are usually eaten with boiled rice.

Clockwise from left:
Making *mee goreng*;
Chicken curry; preparing
belacan; Bok choy

THE HOME KITCHEN

In Malaysia and Singapore the rules of gastronomic tradition are learned in the home kitchen and at the dining table, as are the very tenets of life.

Flip through a few local cookery books and you're likely to find different ingredient lists for even seemingly standard recipes like *kari ayam* (chicken curry). It's only been in recent decades that authors and food historians have embarked upon the precise documentation of the variety of Malaysian and Singaporean foods. The task is a daunting one. For example in, say, Singapore, Penang and Sarawak, laksa has very distinct variants on the same theme. Each is, however, authentic. And how to document dishes from the domestic kitchen? What about a recipe for the ultimate *curry debal?* Such a recipe doesn't exist – one granny's definitive version will be at utter conflict with another auntie's secret recipe.

Rather than stick religiously to recipes, your typical passionate home cook will be more than ready to try out her neighbour's special version, all in the name of improvement (if she can get her hands on it, that is). Social historians may hypothesise that this readiness to adapt can be traced to the migrant mindset. Authorities on gender studies might speculate that it is female home cooks, traditionally cloistered at home, looking for variety. What's for certain is the institution of *agak* (Malay for 'estimation').

Above: A home chef prepares a meal

through painstaking trial and error, acquiring the experience that would prepare them for prospective marriage. Across the many cultures that coexist within these parts, a woman's ability in the kitchen was very seriously regarded as a measure of her desirability as a wife and future mother.

The modern-day kitchen, however, is a very different place. As modernisation occurs, the *kampong* (village) way of life erodes, and women play an increasingly vital role in the world beyond the home, the domestic insularity of yore is no longer. Both husband and wife are likely to put in equally hard hours at work. Dinner can be quickly rustled up or a takeaway bought from a nearby hawker centre. High-density living, particularly in land-scarce Singapore, means economically planned spaces: kitchens are usually large enough to just accommodate a four-plate gas or electric stove, a sink and a few electrical appliances (a rice cooker and a microwave for reheating food being the most common). There is often precious little workspace. Unless already built-in with the apartment, only baking enthusiasts and keen cooks will have a convection oven (although, increasingly, many find the grill/

PASSED DOWN THE GENERATIONS

Cooking is a craft that has always been passed on from generation to generation, typically from mother to daughter. A familial legacy, recipes were not so much instructions set in stone as the passing down of techniques gleaned from observation. Grocery shopping was a daily affair carried out at the crack of dawn in the neighbourhood wet market. Measurements such as grams, tablespoons and

cups were meaningless – learning what a small handful of this, or a generous pinch of that, could constitute helped you learn how to pick out the best from the butcher and vegetable seller, or how to harvest the nicest leaves from the *daun kesum* (laksa leaf) plant in the backyard. You could only gauge how much you needed for your *rempah* (spice paste) when you knew the size and freshness of your lemongrass and chillies. Young girls would hone their skills broiler functions as a close substitute for the charcoal burners of the past). As fridges and freezers are commonplace, food shopping is usually carried out once a week (very often at the supermarket) rather than every day.

Given the harried pace of modern urban life, complex dishes involving labour-intensive preparation and patient simmering are saved for special occasions, celebrations, festivities or convivial gatherings of friends and family. An everyday home-cooked meal will revolve around the staple steamed white rice, served in individual bowls or on plates. Eating with hands or chopsticks has been largely replaced by the fork and spoon. Meat and vegetable dishes (there will be at least two) are served on communal platters in the centre of the table. For ease of use, the lazy Susan is a popular contraption in many homes. Accompaniments that may be laid out on the table include little saucers of *sambal belacan* (chilli and fermented shrimp paste), *cincalok* (fermented shrimps) mixed with a squeeze of lime and thinly sliced shallots, or sliced chillies (red or green) in soy sauce – to say that Malaysians and Singaporeans love their food spicy and savoury is an understatement.

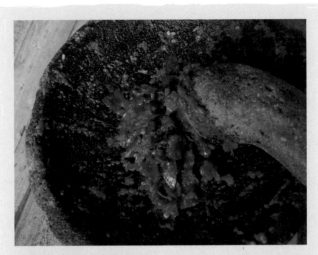

MAKiNG REMPAH

The backbone of many Malaysian and Singaporean dishes is the spice paste rempah. *With a basis of chillies, garlic and shallots, plus a host of other ingredients, it is conventionally prepared with the* batu lesong *(mortar and pestle) or* batu giling *(rectangular grinding stone). Despite the convenience of electric blenders and food processors, dedicated cooks believe nothing can quite replicate the texture of a* rempah *skilfully pounded by hand.*

ESSENTIAL KITCHEN EQUIPMENT

A *kuali*, or wok, is an essential piece of equipment in most homes. While many latter-day variants fashioned from aluminium or stainless steel are readily available, serious cooks still insist on good old-fashioned cast iron. A brand new cast-iron wok needs to be seasoned before use. The Straits Chinese way is to first fry freshly grated coconut in the ungreased wok until the pulp is toasted and dry. The coconut is then discarded and the wok is rinsed. Next, the inner surface of the wok is rubbed all over with the cut side of an onion. The onion is then taken out, bruised and fried in a few tablespoons of vegetable oil. The onion is discarded, the wok is rinsed and it's then ready for use – the more frequently you use the wok, the more seasoned the inner surface becomes and the more 'nonstick' it gets. To clean after use, the wok is simply rinsed with water then wiped thoroughly dry. It is never scoured with steel wool or abrasive agents of any sort as this causes rust.

A new mortar and pestle, hewn from granite or stone, also needs to be seasoned before use. The point is to smooth the inner surface as much as possible. Frequent correct usage is rewarded by an improved ease of use. First, pound sand. Then discard the sand. Then pound vegetable trimmings and peelings, and discard those. Finally, pound raw rice until you get a fine powder. Discard the rice; it will be grey from picking up the grit in the bowl. Repeat the pounding process with raw rice in several batches until the mortar and pestle are smooth, and the resulting rice powder is white in colour.

When stir-frying in a wok, a wide spatula with a long handle is used to toss the ingredients. An assortment of perforated ladles also comes in handy, especially when deep-frying, parboiling or blanching quantities of food such as noodles. These ladles are essentially long-handled strainers, with the best being made of wire mesh with bamboo handles (bamboo is a poor conductor of heat). For steaming, many cooks still use bamboo baskets, specifically designed to fit inside

the wok. Whether used singularly or stacked in multiples, they sit above the simmering water.

Chopping boards are usually substantial wooden affairs and are used for all manner of food preparation. The home kitchen relies on few knives, with the most indispensable being the Chinese cleaver. Usually forged

from carbon steel, the blade is approximately 10cm (4in) wide and 25cm (10in) long. Despite its hefty appearance, it is a truly multipurpose utensil. The blade cuts, chops, slices, shreds, trims, peels, smashes and minces with equal ease.

With rice being a staple food, the electric rice cooker takes the

Above: Chinese cleaver and chopping board

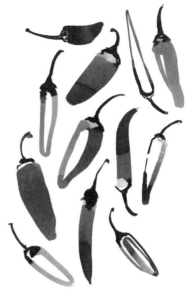

guesswork, trepidation and hassle out of preparing the grain in many a Malaysian and Singaporean household. Hardly anyone cooks rice via the absorption method (which requires much attentiveness) anymore. With a rice cooker, all you need do is throw in the grains, top up with the requisite level of water, and there you have it – perfectly fluffy rice every time.

Aluminium or enamel saucepans and stockpots are used for preparing soups, stocks, braised dishes, stews and curries. It should also be noted that recipes requiring large volumes of coconut milk are not cooked in cast-iron pans because the metal discolours the coconut gravy.

Certain utensils, of course, are culture-specific. An Indian household, for instance, would be in possession of not one but several *blangah* (earthenware vessels for slow-cooked curries) and *tawa* (flat cast-iron griddles). Available in various diameters, *tawa* are used to cook a glorious assortment of *roti* (bread) and *chapati* (griddle-fried breads). On the other hand, a Chinese household wouldn't be without a well-seasoned pot-bellied clay (or sand) pot for sealing in the delicious flavours of a 'red-cooked' dish.

PANTRY ESSENTIALS

Most households keep an array of dried goods, seasonings, flavourings and condiments on standby in the cupboard. Peer into any kitchen cabinet and you'll see candlenuts, cartons or tins of coconut milk, dried red chillies, dried prawns, *belacan*, palm sugar, tamarind pulp and dried tamarind slices, white rice, glutinous rice, dried egg noodles and rice vermicelli. Among the canisters of whole and ground spices, you'll spot cloves, coriander seed, turmeric, cinnamon, cumin, star anise, fennel seed, nutmeg and white and black peppercorns. Sealed in airtight containers or little ziplock bags, these ingredients stay fresh for several months. There will also be the odd commercial packet of ready-mixed curry powder and bottle of spice paste for days when the cook has no energy to start from scratch.

Certain standard ingredients are more culture specific. A Chinese kitchen, say, would also stock tinned bamboo shoots, water chestnuts and straw mushrooms, dried shiitake and cloud-ear mushrooms, *lap cheong* (Chinese preserved pork sausage), salted duck's eggs, dried tangerine peel, Sichuan pepper, five-spice powder, hoisin sauce, and a whole array of fermented black-bean and soya-bean pastes.

Bottles kept within grabbing distance of the stove may include vegetable oil, light and dark soy sauces, *kecap manis* (sweetened dark soy sauce), *shaoshing* (Chinese cooking wine), sesame oil, oyster sauce and black and red Chinese vinegars. In addition, containers of cornflour, salt and sugar aren't too far out of reach. In a tiered wire or plastic basket nearby, there will be heads of garlic and a purple, papery mass of shallots.

In the fridge, small quantities of galangal, ginger, lemongrass, fresh red and green chillies, spring onions, pandan leaf, laksa leaf, curry leaf, fresh coriander, kaffir limes and lime leaf are likely to be spied, each neatly wrapped up in newspaper (which helps absorb moisture and prolongs the shelf life of such perishables).

AT THE MARKET

Markets are a celebration of great produce, culinary fusion and multiculturalism. Offering a glimpse of local life, market shopping is an experience worth getting your feet wet (and your back sweaty) for.

MARKET PRACTICE

Pasar (markets) play a big part in the everyday life of many Malaysians and Singaporeans. The cook of the family sets off early (around 6am) to the market armed with baskets, bags and shopping trolleys to get the best bargains and freshest produce. The market is also a meeting place, where haggling over the freshest produce becomes a social occasion. The atmosphere is almost convivial and bargaining is the norm as shoppers raise the noise quotient by several decibels – even if it's just to knock 10 cents off the price of a bag of *tau geh* (bean sprouts). The stall owners often give as good as they get but, outnumbered by the determined shoppers that descend upon them, they usually concede to shaving a few cents off the initial prices quoted.

A typical market is a one-stop shop sectioned by the kinds of meat, produce and sundries sold. Lining the perimeter of most markets are shops that sell clothes, shoes and other daily necessities like brooms, mops, pails, clothes pegs, pots, pans, cutlery and crockery. Following the general rule of thumb in Malaysia and Singapore, where there is human traffic, there are hawkers and food, so never far away from any market will be a hawker centre or coffeeshop where shoppers can enjoy a cup of *kopi* (coffee sweetened with condensed milk) and a local breakfast before returning to their homes to start the day's cooking.

While neighbourhood markets empty out by mid-morning or noon, there are some central ones that stay open throughout the day to cater to those who prefer to do their shopping after school or work.

WEIGHTS & MEASURES

Malaysia and Singapore both use the metric system of measurements, but you may also come across vendors who still sell based on the traditional Chinese weight measure of kati *(or* catty*), where 1* kati *is equivalent to just under 605g (21.34oz). A* tahil *is one-sixth of a* kati.

PASAR BASAH (WET MARKETS)

Wet markets are so named for their concrete floors that are washed down to clear away dirt and waste, leaving a slopping layer of water lingering on the narrow aisles that separate the stalls. Many stall keepers are decked out in gumboots or galoshes (almost always black or bright yellow), while some opt for wooden clogs. Such footwear is best suited for the slippery floors; if wearing normal shoes, ensure you don't lose your footing while haggling over a piece of fish. Don't be intimidated by the noise and pungent smells of fresh produce mingling in the air. Take a deep breath, dive in and explore. You'll be amply rewarded.

Wet markets are usually divided into distinct sections. Fruit stalls will be located at one end, loaded with stacks of bananas, furry red rambutans, sweet-smelling pineapples, mangoes, apples, oranges and all manner of other tropical fruit. Some stallholders will let you have a taste before you buy.

In the vegetable section, you'll find every possible variation of veggies from local spinach and *daun kari* (curry leaves) to watercress and cabbage. Many vegetables are freshly picked from the market gardens in Malaysia and Singapore, while others come from as far as China and Australia. Look out for things like freshwater chestnuts and other more exotic tubers, roots and leaves, such as young bamboo shoots, turnips and small aubergines (eggplants). Another common sight in the vegetable section is a lady sifting through a pile of bean sprouts removing their dirt and 'tails'.

Not far from the vegetable section will be stalls selling freshly made noodles. These stalls also stock *won-ton* wraps and soya-bean products like silken tofu (soft soya-bean curd, used for cooking) and *tau kee* (dried soy skin used in vegetarian dishes), as well as all sorts of soy sauces and soya beans in their preserved forms. Nearby, eggs – fresh or preserved – can be bought from

Right: Bangsar Sunday market, Kuala Lumpur

stalls that sell them individually or by the carton. Eggs covered in black soot are *ham dan* or *kiam neng* (salted eggs, usually duck), and those in flecks of dark brown sawdust are *pi dan* (century eggs or preserved eggs).

MEAT & FISH STALLS

The wettest part of the wet market is where the meat and fish are sold. If you're squeamish about raw meat and blood, you should avoid this section, where great slabs of meat are hung from hooks and the occasional pig's head or a pail full of entrails shares space with the butchers and their hefty meat cleavers.

Beef, lamb and pork get separate departments in the wet market. And since there is a large Muslim community in both Malaysia and Singapore, halal and haram (forbidden) meats are sold in different sections. For the most part, livestock is slaughtered daily. When choosing your meats look for a good, bright colour and ensure that they are not dry. Note also that ethnic Chinese eat almost every part of an animal, so don't be surprised to see pigs' tongues, trotters, blood and intestines on sale too. Inform the butcher of the cut you want and how much of it, and they will cut it for you; you'll be charged by weight.

Some stalls still sell live poultry and, if you like, you can pick out the plumpest chicken and have it weighed before you go home to chop its head off and pluck its feathers. Alternatively, you can have the stall owner do it for you. For the less adventurous, most other poultry stalls sell ready-cleansed (already-slaughtered) chickens whole or in ready-to-cook cuts. Haram stalls should sell ducks as well. Some stalls sell 'kampong chicken', free-range poultry that tends to be leaner and hence a healthier choice.

At the fish section, you'll find an extensive selection. If you're unsure about what kinds of fish are on display, just quiz the fishmongers, who are a mine of information on these exotic creatures. Among the most highly prized (and highly priced) fish are the *bawal puteh* (silver and white pomfrets) that are best served steamed with chilli, ginger and soy sauce. Large fish like *tenggiri* (mackerel) can be sold whole or in fillets. When choosing, note that fresh fish should be firm to the touch and have shiny scales, red gills and bright eyes. A sure sign that a fish is not fit for consumption are eyes that are cloudy. Some fish stalls also sell homemade fish balls that you can throw into a soup at home.

Piles of *sotong* (squid), *kupang* (mussels) and *udang* (prawns) of all sizes are also readily available. Look for prawns with shiny shells that are not soft and limp. Large baskets or cages of live *ketam* (crabs) are another typical feature at the seafood section. You'll see two main types of crab on sale – the *ketam renjong* (blue swimmer crab or flower crab) that comes from the sea, and the *ketam batu* (mud crab) that lives in the mangrove swamps. Don't miss out on the plethora of shellfish and other fruits of the sea like *kerang* (cockles), *kepah* (Manila clams), *siput* (razor clams), and a popular sea slug used in Chinese cooking called *trepang* (sea cucumber).

Florists also have a home at the wet markets, and they're a cheap source of tropical blooms like heliconias, chrysanthemums and orchids sold by the stalk. The dried-goods stalls line the market's edges, packed with sacks of rice and piles of onions, garlic and dried chillies. These are the stalls to visit if you're looking for packets of *hay bee* (dried shrimp), bottles of soy sauce and oyster sauce, or rice-paper wraps.

MARKET TALK

The language used in the markets of multicultural Malaysia and Singapore represents an entire vocabulary of its own. For example, the Portuguese brought to the Melakan marketplace many new products such as *terung* (aubergine/eggplants), known commonly as *brinjal*. Thanks to the region's colonial history, vegetables are known by their British names rather than their American ones. For example, the crunchy-on-the-outside-slimy-on-the-inside vegetable is called ladies' fingers instead of okra (it's *kacang bendi* in Malay). And because of the mishmash of languages and dialects that locals use, some vegetables have been given entirely new, made-up names like *'ko-le-chai-hua'* for cauliflower: *'ko-le'* is a play on 'cauli', *'chai'* means vegetable, and *'hua'* means flower in simplified Chinese.

Some other foods that are less commonly known by their English names are:

candlenuts	*buah keras*
cardamom	*buah pelaga*
coriander/cilantro	*ketumbar*
lemongrass	*serai*
nutmeg	*buah pala*
fermented soya-bean cakes	*tempeh*
salted soya beans	*tau cheo*
tamarind	*asam*
turmeric	*kunyit*

Clockwise from top left:
Tea eggs are a market snack;
Durian jam at Kota Kinabalu
Night Market; Petaling
Street Night Market

By and large, the wet market is one of the best places to catch an authentic glimpse of local everyday life. All sorts of people trudge through here – bored expats whiling their mornings away, housemaids checking off their shopping lists and happy to have some time away from their employers' homes, harried mothers rushing to buy ingredients for their family meals, old men sitting around a makeshift chequerboard and kids wandering around touching everything in sight. At the end of a long and sweaty shopping trip, the nearby hawker centre beckons with a fine number of local dishes. It may also inspire a second visit to the wet market in an attempt to recreate one of the invariably delicious dishes you will taste.

PASAR MALAM (NIGHT MARKETS)

These open-air market stalls literally spill out onto the pavements at night and tempt you with the sheer variety of goods on sale. As the name suggests, night markets open in the early evening and shut just before midnight – sometimes later, depending on the area. Here you'll find everything from clothes, costume jewellery, CDs and cassettes to toys, grooming products, mattresses, bed linen, food, drink, fruit and much, much more. Come dressed in cool clothing as it can get really hot and sweaty under the bright lights and tarpaulin tents.

Bargaining is the norm at night markets and stall keepers often quote a high price to start off. Don't be shy to haggle them down to what you think is a reasonable price. Stick to your guns and walk away if you have to. More often than not, the stall keeper will back down and accede to the price you've asked for. You'll know you've gone too far when they let you walk away without buying anything. But don't worry as there will surely be another stall selling the same goods not too far down the row.

The highlight of the night market is always the food – and here the prices are fixed. Go on an empty stomach because you'll find an abundance of finger foods like grilled chicken wings, satay (skewers of chicken, mutton or beef grilled over charcoal), skewered fish balls, *otak otak* (spiced fish cakes wrapped in banana leaves and grilled over a charcoal fire) and roasted chestnuts, as well as desserts and sweets like *cendol* (cold coconut-milk dessert), *mua chee* (cooked rice dough shaped into strips, cut into bite-sized pieces and tossed in a chopped peanut and sugar mixture), slices of tropical fruit, and Malay and Peranakan *kuih* (cakes). Some night markets also host their own entertainment with singers crooning hits in Malay, Mandarin, Cantonese and English.

THE WET MARKET is one of the BEST PLACES to catch an authentic GLIMPSE OF LOCAL EVERYDAY LIFE

SPECIALIST ITEMS

Malaysia and Singapore's markets are a treasure-trove of foods and kitchen paraphernalia that you might struggle to find in your home country. And while more esoteric items like mooncake moulds might not see daily use back home, they'll certainly add a spash of Asian charm to your kitchen decor

DRIED SPICES

No wet-market experience would be complete without a visit to the Indian spice stall. These colourful emporia will assault your senses with every imaginable spice from star anise, cumin and cardamom to turmeric, cloves and, of course, curry powder. In large plastic tubs or dishes are the secrets to a good curry and all it takes is a simple request for 'fish curry for two' or 'mutton korma for four'. In a flash of twirling hands, the stall owner will then scoop a little bit of this and that from several tubs into a plastic bag, give it a little shake and hand it over to you for a few cents to a dollar.

KNIVES & UTENSILS

Take the opportunity while you're at a market to buy a good Chinese cleaver; it will set you back a fraction of the cost of a Western-bought equivalent. A knife-sharpening block made of stone is also a good buy and will help keep your blades sharp for a lifetime. Among specialist Peranakan cooking utensils are a *parut*, a special implement for grating coconut, *batu giling* (a grinding stone for making spice pastes) and the bowl-shaped *batu lesong* (mortar and pestle).

COCONUT

Kelapa (coconuts) are essential in local cooking, and the coconut seller usually takes up a small spot near the vegetable section or outside a provision shop. Freshly grated coconut with or without the brown seed coat can be bought here, as well as freshly squeezed coconut cream and milk. This should not be confused with coconut water, which is found inside the young, green coconut when it is opened. *Santan* (coconut milk) is made by squeezing the grated coconut and diluting with water. *Krim kelapa* (coconut cream) is made in the same manner but with less or no water added. Sometimes, a pinch of salt is thrown in to enhance the flavour and help preserve the coconut cream or milk.

AT THE MARKET

WOKS, POTS & BAMBOO STEAMERS

Most Chinese and Malay foods are cooked in a *kuali* (wok), and the market is the best place to find a good-quality one at a reasonable price. Other utensils and cooking equipment to look out for are Indian copper pots, in which curries are best cooked; bamboo steamers that retain heat most effectively; porcelain pots (otherwise known as double-boilers) for double-boiling soups; and Chinese sand and claypots for optimum stewing.

FISH CRACKERS

Crunchy *keropok* (fish crackers, a speciality of the Malay state of Terengganu) are great snacks to take home. They are made from fish and sago flour and seasoned with salt and sugar. Buy them in their dried, uncooked form so when you get home you can fry them in a wokful of vegetable oil to turn them into crispy crackers.

MOULDS & COOKIE CUTTERS

Look out for old-fashioned cake and jelly moulds made of aluminium or sometimes copper that locals use for festive occasions. A favourite for Chinese New Year is a jelly mould in the shape of two carp, which signifies good luck and prosperity. Also pick up wooden-and-net flour sieves and wooden mooncake moulds.

FLAVOURINGS

Belacan (shrimp paste) is a key ingredient when recreating Peranakan dishes at home, and a tub of it can keep for months in the fridge. *Pada* (salt-fish pickle), which is sold in most shops in Melaka, is a great accompaniment to plain rice. *Cincalok* (fermented shrimps) is another Melakan speciality and goes well as a condiment with grilled fish and rice. *Gula melaka* (palm sugar) also keeps for months and is essential when recreating local desserts like sago pudding.

ULAM

To find the unusual selection of herbs and vegetables used in Malay and Peranakan salads, head to the *ulam* stall. Here you'll find fresh ginger, galangal, coriander shoots, lemongrass, fern fronds, *bunga siantan* (torch ginger buds), *daun kaduk* (wild pepper leaf, used in North Malaysian herb-rice dishes), *daun cajus* (young cashew leaves) and the like. The same stall also supplies herbs for soups and drinks, ingredients for betel-leaf chewing, and seasonal fruits like *nangka* (jackfruit), soursop and guava. Also look out for tubers and rhizomes for curries; citruses like *limau kesturi* (calamansi) and the large key lime; and even pickled fish liver and roe preserved in brine.

MEALS

It might seem as if Malaysians and Singaporeans are always eating. In fact, five or six meals or snacks is more the order of the day than strict adherence to the breakfast–lunch–dinner trilogy.

BREAKFAST & MORNING SNACKS

Breakfast is often something that can be grabbed on the run from a roadside or hawker stall on the way to work. The classic Malaysian breakfast is *nasi lemak* (rice boiled in coconut milk served with *ikan bilis* – small, dried sardines or anchovies – peanuts and a curry dish), which can be wrapped to go *(bungkus)* in a banana leaf or brown waxed paper. Also popular are soupy Chinese noodles, delicate *dosa* or soft-boiled eggs and *roti kaya* (toasted white bread spread with *kaya* – coconut and egg sweet spread).

By 10am, it's time for a snack – perhaps a curry puff (a deep-fried pyramid-shaped pastry filled with a dry chicken and potato curry) and a quarter of a hard-boiled egg; or *you char kway* (a deep-fried dough stick) and a *kopi* (local coffee sweetened with condensed milk), which helps tide over the Malaysians' and Singaporeans' insatiable need for a bite until lunchtime.

LUNCH

Lunch hour starts at around 12.30pm and rarely stretches over more than an hour. At the numerous hawker areas dotted across urban centres you'll discover that diners are incredibly focused on scoring themselves a clean table and seat, and they will often hover over seated diners close to ending their meals, seeking to secure a spot before ordering a one-dish meal. Eating is a functional (and, if dining at an outdoor hawker centre, often hot and sweaty) affair at this time of day. It is common for groups of friends and colleagues dining together to share the empty seats at their table with perfect strangers. Everyone's generally out to grab a quick but tasty bite.

Clockwise from far left: *Roti kaya* with eggs for breakfast; Coffee and *you char kway* for afternoon tea; *Ang ku kuih* for supper

DINNER

Dinner spans from sundown until late. Among Malays, there's often a generous time window, with diners lingering over cups of sweet tea, while the Chinese generally tend to approach dinner earlier and more efficiently.

For busy couples and families, dinner is also often eaten at hawker stalls. Meals are more substantial, and diners tend to mix their cuisines, sometimes opting for an Indian salad, a Malay rice dish and a Chinese dessert. Home-cooked dinners, on the other hand, tend to be centred around a single cuisine, usually one traditional to the family. But it's equally common for homemakers to explore and experiment, choosing to pair a spicy-and-sour fish dish with a Chinese clear soup and stir-fried vegetables.

Regular local fare includes stir-fried noodle dishes; Indian *roti canai* served with curry; buffet-style options where diners pick out items from an array at the stall to be served with a portion of rice (Malay, Indian and Chinese stalls have their own versions of this and offer different kinds of dishes); and a host of other hawker favourites. In swankier, air-conditioned food courts such those in shopping malls, expect (along with the local specialities) renditions of Western food such as sandwiches, pizza and burgers, plus Japanese rice sets, Thai noodles and soups, and other foods that reveal the intrinsic openness of local people towards different cuisines.

SUPPER

Late at night, *pasar malam* (night markets) and dedicated street stalls spring up, which in predominantly Malay areas might offer items such as grilled or fried chicken and lots of sweets or, in more diverse areas, Chinese dishes such as fried noodles.

AFTERNOON TEA

The British left behind a strong attachment to afternoon tea, consumed across Malaysia and Singapore in the form of tea or coffee and a sweet or savoury snack like *tong sui* (sweet soup), various Indian fritters, battered and fried slices of cassava, sweet potato or banana and – of course – local-style *kuih* (cakes).

ETIQUETTE

TABLE RULES

As a general rule of thumb, elders should be served first. Within each culture, there is a tradition of welcoming fellow diners to partake of the food with you. Malays say *'jemput makan'* ('please join me'). Always use a serving spoon, not your own spoon, to dish out food, and serve others at the table first before you start on your own meal. And don't forget that Muslims don't eat pork (or consume alcohol), and Hindus and some Buddhists do not eat beef. Serving any of these to staunch believers would be a huge faux pas.

HANDS-ON EATING

At formal Malay dinners and banquets, and at some hawker centres and banana-leaf restaurants, you may notice teapot-like receptacles set atop large, flat-bottomed bowls covered with perforated lids. These are not for your tea and you should not drink the water in them. They are *pembasuk tangan*, finger bowls to be used for washing, should you need to use your fingers to eat.

Always use your right hand to eat. In both Malay and Indian traditions, the right hand is used to give and receive, and to eat. The left hand is considered unclean. The trick to eating elegantly

In Malaysia and Singapore dining out or at home is a relaxed affair. Apart from at the fanciest of restaurants there are no complex cutlery sets to pick your way through, and no slew of wine glasses to leave you guessing which you should drink from next. At nearly all homes and restaurants you'll be provided with a fork and spoon, although few provide knives (most local foods don't require much cutting action). If your host doesn't use chopsticks or eat with his or her fingers, don't ask to do so. A fork and spoon are used nearly all the time, not just in the presence of foreign guests.

with your fingers is to restrict the contact with your food to just the tips of your five fingers. However, remember to use serving spoons, not your fingers, to take food from the communal dish. Indians are said to prefer mixing all the different dishes into their rice, while Malays choose to mix dishes individually into each mouthful of rice. Either way is acceptable. Simply make sure that the food and rice are adequately combined (use the liquids in the curry sauces to help bind them together) before you attempt to raise a mouthful of it to your lips. Here, the trick is to quickly place the ball of rice directly onto your tongue. Watch your neighbours discreetly, and you'll notice that they tend to stick the tips of their tongues out just as they spoon the food in with their fingers.

USING CHOPSTICKS

If you're uncomfortable using chopsticks, it's perfectly acceptable to ask for a fork, either in a home or restaurant setting. However, if you plan on spending any time eating Chinese food, it'll come in handy to practise your chopstick skills. Rounded and tapered on the eating end and square on the holding end, chopsticks are a veritable multi-tool in the right hands – used

for everything from masterfully picking up individual peanuts and mouthfuls of rice to dipping things in sauces, cutting through meat, and holding down a sticky jumble of noodles while someone else takes a small portion.

Start out by making sure your chopsticks are even and that you're holding the right end (the square one). Use your chopsticks to pick up pieces of food, putting them into your own rice bowl first, before bringing them to your mouth. Taking food directly from the serving dish and putting it in your mouth is considered unhygienic.

In some Chinese restaurants and cafes you'll be given a basin of hot water containing bowls, chopsticks and saucers. This is meant to allow for hygiene concerns; remove the items and dry them off or shake them dry.

GREETINGS

Muslims also use only the right hand to 'salaam', or wish one another well. The correct way to do it is to lightly touch as if you're shaking hands and then raise the tips of your fingers on the same hand to your heart. In the case of elders, the younger person kisses the older person's hand, but this is usually reserved for grandparents and aunts and uncles. If a member of the opposite sex fails to *salaam* you, don't be offended. Neither should you pursue the issue. Men generally do not *salaam* women, neither do women *salaam* men.

GIFT GIVING

When visiting someone at home, be sure to bring a gift. Fresh fruit, cakes and other sweet delicacies are ideal. The gift doesn't have to be elaborately packaged, but your host will appreciate a present that comes from the heart. You'll discover that in most families, feeding is an act of love. While Asian cultures do not subscribe to public shows of affection, parents and other family members will articulate their feelings by offering what's perceived as the best parts of any given dish to loved ones. When you are the object of such attention, be sure to eat all that you are given. Waste is frowned upon, and a healthy, appreciative appetite is always much welcomed and admired.

CELEBRATING WITH FOOD

Malaysians and Singaporeans often boast that they live to eat. How fitting then that so many of their major milestones, both personal and public, are marked by great feasts. Every event — from the Chinese New Year to the Muslim Hari Raya Puasa to the Indian Diwali (Deepavali), is a banquet of delights, each unique but equally scrumptious.

Few nations have calendars filled with so many multiethnic rituals and festivals as Malaysia and Singapore –there is rarely a month in these countries' calendars that is devoid of a celebration. And beyond the sheer number of holidays celebrated here, perhaps the most exhilarating thing is that everyone, regardless of cultural origin, takes every festival to be a celebration for all and an excuse to feast. In Malaysia, especially, people commonly open their houses to anyone – even mere acquaintances – when celebrating festivals. At Hari Raya Puasa Muslims welcome all; at Chinese New Year, the Chinese return the favour; and at Christmas and Diwali, Christians and Hindus happily play host. And each group takes it upon themselves to showcase the culinary individuality of their heritage.

TAPAI

Tapai *is a traditional Malay dessert often served at weddings. It's made from sticky rice and gula melaka (palm sugar), touched with powdered yeast and left to its own ageing devices. A cousin in ferment to yogurt,* tapai *is just as good a sweet-and-sour coolant. It numbs the mouth, slakes the thirst and somehow feels healthily indulgent.*

Above: *Yee sang*, a traditional Chinese New Year dish

WEDDINGS

No occasion in Malaysia and Singapore brings people together better than a wedding. Locals love weddings, both for what they represent but also for the banquets that follow. Although modern couples now prefer to host banquets at hotels, traditional weddings can span days of feasting. Much of the food bears symbolic significance. A Peranakan mother-in-law, for example, may present a special *nasi lemak* (coconut rice) to the mother of her son's bride, to acknowledge that the bride is a virgin. At Malay weddings, guests are presented with ornate, beautifully packaged gifts of hard-boiled eggs when they leave – a wish for fertility and offspring.

CHINESE ENGAGEMENT CEREMONY

On an auspicious day picked out from the Chinese almanac by the couple's parents or relatives, the groom visits the bride's house, paying his respects and 'bargaining' for her hand. This can involve anything from answering silly questions about her to the actual exchange of money. Once accepted, the groom takes the bride to his home, where they go down on their knees to serve his parents and older relatives a specially brewed tea. The whole ceremony acts as symbol for the young bride's acceptance to serve and care for her new relatives. The groom's family usually brings gifts of food to the bride's parents – a whole roasted suckling pig coloured red is a traditional offering.

Anything up to 1000 guests are expected at a Malay wedding, where the feasting traditionally starts at 11am and stretches on to 5pm. Throughout the day, guests stop by to convey their good wishes, and stay for a meal of *nasi minyak* (a rice dish cooked with *ghee* – clarified butter – and spices) or *biryani dam* (an Indian and Arabic speciality where the rice and meat is laid out layer upon layer), with a *kari ayam* (chicken curry) and beef *rendang*. Cooking for such huge numbers is a time-consuming affair and the elected chefs set up a makeshift open-air kitchen (most

LUCKY DISHES

Typically, Chinese wedding banquets include eight or nine dishes. The Mandarin word for eight, ba, sounds like the word for good luck, while the word for nine, jiu, sounds like the word for long. Serving eight or nine dishes is a way to invoke good luck and longevity for the newlyweds.

weddings are held in open, communal spaces) at least a day ahead. The cooking sometimes goes through the night, and someone must spend the night simply watching over the food!

Similarly, at an Indian wedding, the food section presents a veritable feast – biryani (steamed rice oven-baked with meat, vegetables and spices) at a Muslim wedding, *macher tarkari* (fish curry) at a Bengali one and *murg makhanwala* (butter chicken) at a Punjabi do. And the festivities can span days.

CHINESE WEDDING BANQUETS

A Chinese wedding banquet is both a joy and a stress-inducing, logistical nightmare. As times have changed, banquets have become as much about celebrating a young couple's love for each other, as they are opportunities for proud parents to show off to friends. Further, in Malaysia and Singapore, people often speak of 'wedding face', which lies behind the trend towards larger and larger banquets. Quite simply, 'wedding face' means that if you have been invited to someone's child's wedding, you are honour-bound to invite them to your child's; to not do so is a loss of face, something Chinese take very seriously. High-society wedding banquets are often attended by up to 1000 people – some are even held over several nights.

The banquet itself is a multicourse Chinese food extravaganza, usually held at a hotel or a restaurant. In the past, shark's fin soup was a staple dish; parents ordered it not only because it was delicious but also because it demonstrated wealth. These days, couples are taking shark's fin off their nuptial celebration menus for both ethical and budget concerns. That said, most dinners usually offer eight or nine courses – anything less is considered 'cheap'. The first courses are often served with a sound-and-light show, a chance for the venue to show off its innovative packaging and hopefully attract more weddings to be booked with them.

Toasts are also common at these events. Chinese love to toast and do so by bringing their glasses of whisky, cognac or more recently, red wine, together and yelling '*yam seng*' – a Cantonese term that literally means 'drink to victory'. More specifically, they yell '*yam*' for as long as they can, followed by an emphatic '*seng*', after which the glass is downed.

At the close of the banquet, the happy couple and their parents line up, forming a farewell party at the doorway, signalling the end of the evening with their desire to personally thank all their guests. At big weddings, smart guests get up quickly; you can only imagine how long it takes to shake 1000 pairs of hands.

BIRTHDAY TREATS

To celebrate births across most cultures in Malaysia and Singapore, the baby's first month is marked with a banquet. On the 100th day, some Chinese families cook a chicken and its tongue is rubbed on the baby's lips to ensure the child will be an eloquent speaker.

To mark each progressive birthday, most locals throw a party and take it as an excuse to tuck into a good meal. Some classic traditions, however, do remain. In Peranakan and Chinese families, for example, the birthday person is served *yi mein* (longevity noodle). The noodles symbolise long life and they are often paired with hard-boiled eggs, representing fertility or life.

Shou tao (longevity peach buns), shaped like peaches and filled with red-bean or lotus-seed paste, are another enduring favourite. Peaches and peach trees have always been symbolic; it is believed that bad spirits fear peach wood and pits. Chinese also believe that peaches symbolise springtime and beauty.

A FOOD CALENDAR

Muslim holidays follow a lunar calendar, while dates for Chinese and Hindu religious festivals are calculated using the lunisolar calendar. Muslim holidays fall around 11 days earlier each year, while Hindu and Chinese festivals change dates but fall roughly within the same months.

JANUARY

PONGOL
This Hindu festival, which usually takes place in mid-January, celebrates the end of the harvest season. *Pongol*, either a sweet or salty rice dish made in a claypot, is prepared and Hindu temples see various festivities over a four-day period.

Left: New Year lanterns at Thean Hou Temple, Kuala Lumpur

FEBRUARY

CHINESE NEW YEAR

Marking the coming of spring, this festival was once the only time Chinese farmers took a break from working the fields. These days, few Malaysian and Singaporean Chinese are farmers, and the holiday represents more of a spiritual renewal than a physical one – offering new beginnings, new opportunities and a reaffirmation of family ties.

For most of the traditional 15-day celebrations, which either start in late January or early February depending on the year, Chinese New Year practices remain similar to those in mainland China: Malaysian and Singaporean Chinese clean their homes to get rid of last year's dust and misfortunes; settle all debts; buy new clothes and shoes; and visit one another bearing good wishes and to exchange *hong bao* (lucky red envelopes filled with money).

There are, however, other traditions unique to the region. On New Year's Day, visitors are often offered titbits: orange segments for good luck, and sweets and cookies for a sweet future. Peranakans have added 'love letters', wafer-thin biscuits otherwise known as *kuih Belanda* (Dutch cake), to the selection. The round, sweet, thin-and-crispy rice-powdered wafers are rolled up in little scrolls or folded in fourths to look like unfolded Chinese fans. They are time-consuming to make. The round shape of an unfolded love letter is significant. The Chinese character for round, '*yuan*', also means satisfaction or a cycle of life, so the round love letter therefore connotes success in one's cycle of life.

Ayam siyow (chicken in tamarind sauce), another Peranakan Chinese New Year favourite, grew out of more pragmatic needs. As shops and markets often stayed shut during the festivities, and refrigerators were once a rarity, Peranakans would buy several chickens and cook them with spices, using tamarind to preserve the meat. They thus had a handy dish that could be served during any meal.

But the practice that differentiates Singapore from Malaysia is the belief in eating *yu sheng*, a salad of paper-thin raw fish, finely grated vegetables, candied melon and lime, red and white pickled ginger, pomelo sacs, sesame seeds, jellyfish and peanuts tossed in a dressing. It's eaten on the seventh day of the New Year, when Singaporean families and, more often, business associates, first toss the salad with their chopsticks, shouting '*lo hei*' (toss the fish) – a wish for rising prosperity and abundance – before they eat it. The recipe for *yu sheng* is said to have been created in Singapore in the 1960s (although other sources have it being invented at a Chinese restaurant in Malaysia's Serembam during the 1940s). Special qualities are attributed to each ingredient, and the dish's name sounds like the phrase 'rising abundance' in Chinese. With a tradition filled with dishes consumed for their auspicious names, Chinese find *yu sheng* appealing, and a way they can eat their way into a prosperous New Year. This practice has now spread to Malaysia and Hong Kong. But it is in Singapore that it is religiously consumed.

MAY

DUAN WU JIE (DRAGON BOAT FESTIVAL)

Celebrated on the fifth day in the fifth month of the lunar calendar (which falls from mid-May to mid-June), this festival marks the death of Chinese patriot-scholar Qu Yuan, who committed suicide by drowning in Hunan's Milo River in 278 BCE. The local people, who admired Qu Yuan, raced out in their boats to save him, or at least retrieve his body – from this came the tradition of dragon boat racing. The people also threw sticky rice wrapped in bamboo leaves into the river so that the fish would eat the rice instead of his body. Hence, bamboo-wrapped rice dumplings (known as *bak chang*) stuffed with meat, chestnuts and mushrooms, among other dishes, are eaten in his memory leading up to the day of the festival.

JUNE

GAWAI DAYAK FESTIVAL

This week-long festival marks the end of the paddy-harvesting season for the Dayaks (tribal peoples) of Sarawak. Officially, it falls on 1 and 2 June, but the ceremony starts days earlier and stretches well into the month. Observed by Sarawak's Iban and Bidayuh communities, the festival involves much merrymaking, dancing and the drinking of *tuak* (a potent rice wine) in addition to cockfights, war dances and blowpipe competitions. To eat are exotic delicacies such as *tempoyak* (fermented and near-alcoholic durian pulp) and *ikan kasam* (fermented preserved fish with black beans).

SEPTEMBER

MID-AUTUMN FESTIVAL

Also known as the Mooncake Festival, this is observed by Chinese on the 15th day of the eighth lunar month (which falls either in September or October) as a celebration of autumn harvests. The traditional style of *yue bing* (mooncakes) savoured at this time are made of baked pastry filled with either sweet *hong dou* (red bean) or *lian rong* (lotus seed) paste and studded in their centre with *xian ya dan huang* (salted duck-egg yolks). In

Left: Mooncakes for the Mid-Autumn Festival

OCTOBER

DIWALI (DEEPAVALI)

Hindus celebrate Diwali, the Festival of Lights marking the triumph of good over evil, on the new moon of the seventh month of the Hindu calendar (usually in October or November). Rows of earthenware oil lamps are lit to welcome Lakshmi, goddess of wealth, and a vast variety of Indian dishes are created for the occasion. *Muruku* (a deep-fried noodle-like snack made of rice and lentil flours), *dosa* (paper-thin rice-and-lentil crêpes) and *putu mayam* (string hoppers, or rice noodles) are just some of the delicacies painstakingly prepared for friends and relatives who join in the festivities.

fancier Malaysian and Singaporean bakeries and hotels, it's now common to find mooncakes filled with pandan; or Teochew-style cakes with a crust made from lighter filo pastry, filled with green or red beans or yam.

Look out too for unbaked snowskin mooncakes with crusts made from glutinous rice and with a texture similar to mochi. Less oily than traditional mooncakes, this type needs to be chilled and often comes in fruit flavours such as durian. They also may be alcohol-infused.

DECEMBER

CHRISTMAS

Despite the heat, shopping malls and department stores in Singapore and across Malaysia are covered in twinkling fairy lights and fake snow in the run up to Christmas. The best indication of how nondenominational the celebration has become in the region is the growing tradition of serving roasted turkey stuffed with a mixture of glutinous rice, braised pork and chestnuts. This stuffing is usually used to make *bak chang* (dumplings associated with the Chinese Dragon Boat Festival). Whole honey-baked hams and log or fruit cakes are also commonplace, although they are likely to be paired with a *kari ayam* (chicken curry) or *popiah* (Peranakan spring rolls that are not deep-fried).

While house parties with friends are aplenty in the weeks leading up to Christmas Day, Christmas dinner itself is a family affair. A unique Christmas meal culturally specific to this region is the Eurasian dinner. For Eurasians, who are usually Catholic, Christmas is a major festival marked by hours slaving over a hot stove to create holiday specials such as *curry debal* (devil curry, incorporating ingredients such as ham, luncheon meat or sausages); *feng* (a pork curry and Christmas speciality that is best eaten a day old); roasts basted with a soy-sauce-based marinade and served with chilli dips; Eurasian chicken pies; *coubes gulung* (Kristang for stewed cabbage rolls); and *sugee* cake (a moist, ultra-sweet sponge cake). Families traditionally head for Midnight Mass before returning home, at 2am, to a table laden with these Eurasian delicacies and a turkey fresh out of the oven.

RAMADAN

One of the tenets of Islam is Ramadan, a compulsory month-long fast where faithful Muslims abstain from eating, drinking, smoking and other sensory pleasures from dawn to dusk. Don't worry if you're a visitor during this time: restaurants, cafes and bars stay open through the day, but you may find some of the Malay workers and owners a little sluggish through the daily fasting.

As dusk approaches, families flock to Ramadan night markets in which stalls offer all manner of ready-cooked, delicious foods to be taken home or eaten immediately after sundown by the ravenous. Hotels and restaurants also put on sumptuous, all-you-can-eat *iftar* buffets: *iftar* is the breaking-of-the-fast meal after sunset during Ramadan. It's worth searching out these markets and buffets to sample the wide range of local Malay delicacies.

HARI RAYA PUASA

Hari Raya Puasa marks the end Ramadan, falling on the first day of Syawai (the 10th month in the Muslim calendar). Hari Raya means 'a great day', and Puasa is derived from Sanskrit meaning 'fasting or abstention'. So Hari Raya Puasa actually means 'the festival marking the end of a period of fasting'. The festival is also known as Eid al-Fitr, Arabic for 'breaking of the fast'.

The day begins with prayers in the mosques for the men and visits to cemeteries followed by a substantial brunch. The women, who pray at home, spend their time preparing the brunch. The meal usually consists of *ketupat* (rice cakes wrapped in coconut leaves), beef *rendang* (beef in a thick coconut-milk curry sauce), *sambal goreng* (prawns, meat and soya-bean cake cooked in chilli and coconut milk) and *serunding* (desiccated coconut fried with chilli). For the rest of the day, friends and family visit one another and guests are pampered with every type of dish, cake, biscuit and delicacy imaginable. These days, dishes are exchanged between neighbours to the point where tables groan under the weight of food. The food is usually accompanied by tea, coffee, syrupy drinks (rose-flavoured ones are favoured) and soft drinks.

GUESTS ARE **PAMPERED** *with every type* OF DISH, CAKE, BISCUIT AND **DELICACY** *imaginable*

WHERE & HOW to EAT

In Malaysia and Singapore it's possible to snack, sup or sip round practically every street corner. To eat or drink here is far more than an act of sustenance, it is a social experience – a chance to let your taste buds savour the cultural melange of these two countries.

© Phil Weymouth | Lonely Planet

54

Listen to locals when they tell you that the best food is found at the compact little kitchens-on-wheels that line alleyways and pavements, fill whole hawker enclaves, and cluster around popular *kopitiam* (coffeeshops). In the region's bigger cities, there's a good spread of everything, including many international options; in the smaller and more rural towns and villages, the choice will narrow down to Malay, Chinese and perhaps Indian cuisine. Usually only the high-end restaurants in the major cities require advance booking.

PLACES TO EAT

HAWKER STALLS

Enjoy super-fresh, tasty and affordable meals at these street-side stalls, sometimes gathered in clusters to cater for customers of day and night markets.

FOOD COURTS

Often found in air-conditioned shopping malls, food courts are essentially air-conditioned hawker centres with marginally higher prices.

KOPITIAM

Old-style Chinese coffeeshops, these simple, fan-cooled establishments serve noodle and rice dishes, strong coffee and other drinks, and all-day breakfast fare like soft-boiled eggs and toast spread with *kaya* (coconut jam).

RESTORAN (RESTAURANTS)

Restaurants range from casual, decades-old Chinese establishments to upscale places boasting international fare, slick decor and a full bar.

PASAR (MARKETS)

Morning markets usually have Chinese-owned stalls selling coffee and Indian-operated *teh tarik* stalls offering freshly griddled *roti*. Triangular *bungkus* (packages) piled in the middle of tables contain *nasi lemak* (coconut rice); help yourself and pay for what you eat. At *pasar malam* (night markets) you'll find everything from laksa to fresh-fried doughnuts.

MENUS

Deciphering menus in Malaysia and Singapore is a cinch. Most locals speak some English; at hawker stalls, basic sign language and polite pointing generally gets your order across. Your biggest problem will be deciding what to order from the many delicious dishes on offer.

When attempting to dive headlong into the food culture of Malaysia and Singapore, don't be afraid to ask a fellow diner for his or her help and advice. Food-loving locals tend to be only too happy to oblige. You'll invariably spot curious diners indiscreetly peering at their neighbour's table as dish after scrumptious-looking dish is carried to it. It's quite acceptable to peer, point and stare in most outdoor and casual eateries. Just remember to put on your friendliest smile. And if driven to desperation, you can quite easily order yourself a fabulous meal by asking for whatever looks good at the next table!

IN RESTAURANTS

Most, if not all, restaurants have menus printed in English, which will be offered to you when you are seated. If the menu contains names of local dishes in Malay or Chinese, an English description of the dish will follow, more often than not.

À la carte menus are offered at most restaurants. In Chinese (and some Malay) restaurants, dishes are often categorised under food groups, ie, appetisers, poultry, beef, seafood, vegetables, soups, noodles and rice. As Asian meals are traditionally communal, it would be best to order several dishes to sample and share. Most Chinese and Malay restaurants offer dishes in small, medium and large portions. Be sure to indicate your preference to the serving staff. If you are unsure, they should be able to make recommendations.

As a rough guide, single servings are sufficient as a one-dish meal for one person, when paired with a serving of rice. However, the general rule of thumb for couples is to order no more than three different dishes to share.

AT HAWKER STALLS

At hawker centres and food courts, menus are generally displayed on a signboard above the stalls or on the storefront's glass display cases. These menus often state, quite simply, the names of the dishes, some in English, some not. If you are unsure, ask the stall's vendor or, if the vendor doesn't speak English, any of the patrons around the stall. Most locals speak some English, are proud of their local cuisine and will be happy to provide you with a lowdown on the various dishes and what they contain. Some stalls also display photographs of their dishes to help you along. Otherwise, simply watch as the chef throws together another diner's order and decide whether you like the look of the dish.

When attempting to place your order, though, be sure to jump right in there and catch the vendor's attention. Get in line if there is a queue. If there isn't one, ask if anyone else is waiting to place an order. If no-one is, be assertive and go up to the vendor and tell him or her exactly what you want (they're usually too busy and harried to pause and ask you for your order).

Feel free to ask for more or less chilli, or request that other elements of the dish to be adjusted to your liking. Try to make eye contact. You don't want the chef to forget what you ordered or who they should deliver the dish to once it's done. Some hawker-centre tables have numbers on them. Remember your number before placing an order, as the vendor will ask you for it so they can send your food to the right table. At places where tables aren't numbered, point in the general direction of your seat and rest assured that the vendor will find you; they usually manage to send the right order to the right table. But to be safe, keep an eye out for the delivery person and wave at them if you think it's your dish they're holding.

Don't feel obliged to order from just one stall. The point of hawker centres is that patrons get to order from as many stalls as they like and sample a variety of local fare. Also note there are some self-service stalls that require you to take your own dishes to the table (a sign stating so will be prominently displayed on the stall). If there are no vacant tables at hawker centres, food courts and traditional coffeeshops, sharing a table with strangers is not a problem. In fact, it can be the perfect way to strike up a conversation about food. Simply ask, before you sit down, whether the seats are taken. If the people already occupying part of the table don't understand English, pointing at the seats and nodding would suffice. A friendly smile goes a long way, of course.

ECONOMY RICE & MIXED RICE

At some hawker centres, you'll find stalls that sell an array of

CHEF RECOMMEND
厨师好介绍
Roasted Peking Duck
北京烤填鸭
Deep Fried "Soon Hock" Fish
油浸顺壳鱼
Whampoo Quick Boiled
Noodles With Prawns
黄埔虾球捞面
Chilli Crab
辣椒螃蟹

From far left:
Hawker stall dishes in Singapore; Fried tofu, spring rolls and fish balls with chilli sauce; Menu board

cooked dishes, such as curries, fried vegetables, fried chicken wings and *sambals* (chilli-based condiments), all displayed on glass shelves. Chinese know this arrangement of dishes by its Hokkien name, *chap chye peng* (economy rice), while Malays call their version *nasi campur*, Indonesians *nasi padang* and Indians *nasi kandar*. These stalls charge a standard amount for three dishes (two meats and one vegetable) on a plate of rice and then charge extra for any other dish you might choose to add. Generally, the vegetable dishes are the cheapest while the beef tend to be the most expensive. Feel free to ask about the price of each dish before ordering as these stalls don't usually have a written menu. Instead, simply point at the dishes you want and the vendor will pile your choices onto a plate of rice.

PRICES
Prices at hawker stalls and restaurants are fixed and the menus should state the price of your dish. If they don't, then you're likely to be in a tourist trap. If you think you're getting ripped off, ask any of the local diners around you what you should be paying and they should be happy to tell you.

61

HAWKER STALLS & CENTRES

The hawker meal is central to the experience of eating here. This is how most locals dine on a regular basis. Even after a splendid dinner at home, people may even choose to head out to their favourite supper joints for an extra hawker fix!

HAWKER ORIGINS

The original food hawkers carried their wares on their backs, balancing two bundles consisting of foodstuff and equipment, on either end of a pole swung over their shoulders. They would set up shop at busy street corners and at plantations where hungry labourers sought quick, hearty meals. Alternatively, they simply took to the streets, announcing their presence by the tok-tok of short bamboo sticks tapped against one another (which explains why they were also called tok-tok vendors), only stopping when an order was placed.

Dishes were assembled on the spot. Some hawkers had more elaborate equipment – satay vendors would set up stoves and grill their sticks of chicken, mutton and beef over a charcoal fire. Customers would come to the makeshift stall bearing their own plates and bowls. But this is a tradition that has all but disappeared.

Clockwise from left:
'Satay Street' in Singapore's Lau Pa Sat hawker centre; An old-fashioned food cart in Penang; Hawkers serving up in Singapore

HAWKERS TODAY

More common now are pushcart stalls with fires powered by large gas canisters. Some remain in one spot all the time, others move from place to place. Many gather at an agreed location, and set up tables and chairs for their shared diners (often in the open air). Chances are, you'll find one or two close to, or situated right in, major markets in each town. Some street hawkers associate themselves with coffeeshops with indoor seating, others offer minimal seating built into their carts, and some don't offer seats of any sort!

Hawker centres serve hawker food, but do so in purpose-built structures with basic services such as electricity, running water and washrooms provided. There are many tables, and you are likely to find a greater selection of food.

Huge efforts have been made to raise the hygiene standards of hawker food preparation by moving hawker carts off the streets and into permanent stalls at hawker centres and food courts; in Singapore stand-alone hawker carts have almost disappeared. But they are common throughout Malaysia, and many pushcart stallholders will position themselves close to popular eating establishments, tapping into their pool of diners.

Of course, popular pushcart stalls similarly help entice diners into choosing to stop at the coffeeshops they associate themselves with. Often, for a small table charge, the coffeeshop will allow you to eat the hawker food in their establishment – especially if the pushcart stall itself offers no tables and seats.

HAWKER MEALS

Most significant of all is the fact that the hawker meal best reflects the multicultural nature of Malaysia and Singapore. No meals need be cuisine-specific. You can choose to start with an Indian-Muslim *rojak* (deep-fried vegetables and seafood served with spicy-sweet sauce, and fresh cucumber, tomato and onion), go on to tuck into a Chinese *char kway teow* (broad, flat rice-flour noodles stir-fried with Chinese sausage and egg in a sweet, dark soy sauce) with a side dish of Malay *sop ekor lembu* (oxtail soup), then complete your meal with a Coke and an *ais kacang* (a Malaysian shaved ice dessert). Diners can choose to eat communally the way most Asians do, or simply order a single portion of what they feel like eating.

Most hawker dishes are designed as single portions – a bowlful of noodles in soup, a plateful of fried rice or noodles, a single serving of dessert. But there are exceptions to the rule. Most stallholders expect vegetable dishes like *kerabu taugeh* (bean sprout salad), and meat dishes like satay (spicy grilled-meat skewers) to be shared. Some rice dishes such as chicken rice can be ordered in portions suited to the number of diners sharing the meal – meaning that you'd get a serving of chicken on one plate placed in the middle of the table, with individual plates of rice for each diner. The important thing to note is that most stalls specialise in only one dish.

Left: Hawker cooking satay
on grill at Lau Pa Sat hawker
centre, Singapore

HAWKER ETIQUETTE

*Bag a seat first, especially if it's busy. Sit a
member of your group at a table, or 'chope'
(Singaporean slang for 'save' or 'reserve')
your seat by laying a packet of tissues there.
Don't worry if there are no completely free
tables; it's normal to share with strangers.*

*• If there's a table number, note it as the stall
owner uses it as a reference for food delivery.*

*• If the stall has a 'self service' sign, you'll
have to carry the food to the table yourself.
Otherwise, the vendor brings your order to
you.*

*• Ignore wandering touts who try to sit you
down and plonk menus in front of you.*

*• It's customary to return your tray once
finished, although there are a few roaming
cleaners who'll take your empty dishes.*

RICE STALLS

There are two kinds of rice stalls: those that offer a
wide selection of dishes to accompany your rice (you
tell them what you want) and those that simply serve
a specific kind of meat with rice.

Nasi lemak (coconut rice, usually served for
breakfast with fried fish), *nasi campur* (rice with
Malay dishes), *nasi padang* (the Indonesian version,
pretty much identical to *nasi campur*), *nasi kandar*
(the Indian version) and *chap chye peng* (the Chinese
version, sometimes referred to as economy rice)
stalls fall under the former category. Pick the kind of
rice you prefer (at economy-rice stalls you'll only get
plain steamed rice; at the others, you're likely to get
a choice of plain rice, coconut rice or possibly *nasi
kuning* – rice cooked with turmeric powder and other
spices), then let your fingers do the pointing.

The other kind of rice stall is either a chicken-
rice stall, or a roasted or barbecued pork and duck
stall – sometimes all these meats are served at the
same stall. These are usually identified by the rows
of whole cooked chicken, roasted duck, slabs of
crisp, roasted belly pork and lengths of *char siew*
(barbecued pork) displayed in its window. Depending
on whether you're ordering a dish for one person
or more, the meat you've chosen will be sliced and
placed on top of a serving of rice (if just for one diner)
or placed on a separate dish to be shared between
diners (if for more than one). The meat will usually
come heaped over cucumber slices, but at some stalls
it also comes over side orders of stir-fried vegetables.
A bowl of clear chicken soup customarily comes with
the meal.

PICK 'N' MIX STALLS

At these type of stalls, which offer one serving of Chinese food and a salad dish called *rojak* (meaning 'mixed' in Malay), you can choose the different elements of your meal. There is usually a stack of empty bowls or plates placed to one side of the display. Diners help themselves to a plate and a pair of tongs and pick the items that they like. Watch to see what the people ahead of you do. Some stallholders prefer to pick up the items themselves as you point to them.

Derived from the Hokkien words for cooking and frying, *tze char* (sometimes spelled *cza char* or *zi char*) is a uniquely Singaporean dining term referring to stalls selling an extensive mish-mash of dishes cooked to order, based loosely on Chinese cooking, with plenty of Malay, Indian and Peranakan influences. *Tze char* stalls typically open only at dinner time, and many operate late into the night. You'll notice that some stalls have beautiful displays of fried rolls, meat and fish balls, stuffed chillies, tofu and other bits and pieces.

Rojak consists of pieces of hardboiled egg, tofu, fried fish cake and other specialities which are often deep-fried again right after you've picked them out, cut into bite-sized pieces and then served with a spicy-sweet dip. Note that the Penang style of *rojak* is more of a salad, made of pineapple, turnip and cucumber slices tossed in a sauce made with shrimp paste, dried shrimp, dark sauce, chillies and ground peanuts (you don't get to pick the ingredients for this).

Lor bak is similar to *rojak* in that it's also deep-fried and served with a dip. But *lor bak* stalls also offer a selection of liver and shrimp rolls (wrapped in *tau kee* – bean curd skin – and deep-fried) and other meats dipped in batter and then fried. *Yong tau fu* stalls boast a broad selection of fish balls, tofu cubes stuffed with minced pork, bitter gourd slices and green chillies stuffed with fish paste; you can choose to have these in a clear soup, with *bee hoon* (rice vermicelli) and *kangkong* (water spinach), or dry, served over *bee hoon* and doused in a sweet-and-savoury sauce.

Left: Pick 'n' mix your lunch in Singapore
Right: Noodles at Kimberley Street Food Night Market, George Town

NOODLE STALLS

The rhythmic scraping of metal spatula against the sides of a wok is a clear indication that you're nearing a fried noodle stall. But what type of *mee* (noodle) dish is being served? With some practice you'll learn to tell, by the sweet aroma in the air, what kind of noodles are being prepared. Does it have the smell of caramelised sweet dark sauce and fatty Chinese sausage? That would be *char kway teow*. Or perhaps there's the scent of seafood plus the tangy bouquet of freshly squeezed calamansi (a small, round lime)? It's got to be fried *Hokkien mee* (a stir-fried dish filled with squid, tiny shrimp, pork and vegetables). An eggy spiciness coupled with the smell of cabbage cooking? That's *mee goreng* (a spicy fried-noodle dish).

But if there's no hot wok action, and all the hawker has is a steaming cauldron of soup, then you're heading towards soupy-noodle territory, which just means that the noodles are cooked in boiling hot water and served either in a broth or dry with the broth on the side. Variations abound. Hokkien prawn *mee* soup usually consists of *Hokkien mee* (thick egg noodles) in a rich prawn broth topped with cooked prawns, while prawn *mee* is the same noodles tossed in a spicy sauce and topped with cooked prawns. *Bak chor mee* is noodles doused with Chinese black vinegar and the hawker's special sauce, then topped with minced pork, fish balls, pickles, freshly chopped spring onions and toasted dried fish. *Wonton mee* or *char xiu mee* is a soup featuring delicate *wontons* (dumplings) filled with minced pork, Chinese mushrooms and water chestnuts, plus thin slices of barbecued pork, egg noodles and chopped spring onions.

CHAI TOW KWAY

A popular stir-fried hawker dish in the region is chai tow kway, *also called* char kway kak *in Singapore. It's known in English as fried radish or fried carrot cake, although it's nothing like a western carrot cake! The steam-cooked cake is made from grated daikon radish mixed with rice flour. Chunks of the cake are then stir-fried with various veggies and eggs to give them a crispy coating. A 'black' version of the dish adds sweet dark soy sauce.*

Idli are steamed rice-flour and lentil cakes that look like little flying saucers (they are steamed in shallow moulds). They can be eaten with coconut chutney and *sambar* (spicy vegetable and lentil stew), with a mango or onion chutney, or even with just sweetened coconut milk.

Appam or hoppers are fermented rice cakes. You'll spot a stall selling them by the row of tiny woks lined-up in a row. Each pan is just big enough for one *appam* – it has a thin, delicate outer ring that's fairly crisp, and a thicker, moist centre. Eaten sprinkled with brown sugar, it makes a scrumptious breakfast or snack.

INDIAN RICE—FLOUR SNACK STALLS

Often in Indian areas of cities such as Kuala Lumpur, George Town, Melaka and Singapore you'll come across stalls selling the following South Indian specialities, which are eaten as snacks or for breakfast.

Idiappam is otherwise known as string hoppers and looks like steamed rice vermicelli. Served as a disc of fine netting, it is either eaten with brown sugar and grated coconut or with a curry.

ROTI (BREAD) STALLS

The first thing that should catch your eye is the huge griddle at the counter. First thing in the morning at the *roti canai* stall, you'll see the stallholder kneading his dough, slapping it onto the counter-top and pinching it into individual portions. Like a pizza chef, he flicks his ball of dough into the air, effortlessly stretching it into a thin disk which he then folds into itself. The resulting flaky flatbread is pan-fried on a griddle.

Traditional versions of this pan-fried bread include the plain *roti canai* (also known as *roti prata* in Singapore) sprinkled with sugar or served with curry sauces, *roti telur* (with an egg cracked into the middle) and *roti bawang telur* (with egg and fried sliced onions). *Murtabak* is a heavier version with the *roti* dough sandwiching spiced minced mutton or chicken, somewhat reminiscent of lasagne. Of course, modern variations have been created, including *roti pisang* (filled with banana) and *roti Planta* (with a thick layer of margarine; Planta is a popular brand of the spread).

DOSA

A dosa (also spelled dosai*) is a large, paper-thin rice-and-lentil crêpe that is made by ladling the batter onto a lightly greased dosa pan. Plain dosa are served with tomato and onion chutney, coconut chutney and yellow* daal *(cooked lentils). Vengaya dosa (onion dosa) has fried onions sprinkled over it. Masala dosa is filled with a dry, spicy potato filling, then folded into a triangular package.*

Above: A hawker prepares *murtabak*

Below: Barbecued chicken wings
Right: Malay-style *curry mee*

SATAY

Depending on your appetite satay can be a meal on its own. Marinated pieces of chicken, beef and mutton are threaded onto bamboo sticks before they are grilled over a charcoal fire. Other more exotic satay options include turkey, chicken feet, cow intestines, chicken cartilage and duck liver. Chinese also enjoy pork satay, which is easily identifiable by the layers of fat that is left in-between the pork flesh.

Satay is sold by the stick and served with a spicy peanut dip, ketupat (pressed rice cooked in a case made from coconut fronds), and perhaps chunks of cucumber and slices of raw onion and/ or pineapple. Once you've eaten the meat from your bamboo skewer, use the skewer to pick up the accompaniments.

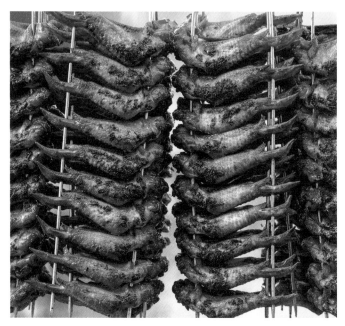

GRILLED DISHES STALLS

Barbecued chicken wings are extremely popular. You'll find stalls just selling chicken wings served with wedges of calamansi and a dollop of chilli sauce. You will be able to identify these stalls by their rather unique barbecue and skewer contraptions, specially designed by the hawkers themselves to be able to maximise the number of chicken wings that can go over the charcoal fire at any given time.

Also very popular is *ikan bakar* (grilled fish). Grilled *pari nyiru* (stingray) slathered in *sambal* (a chilli-based condiment) and served on a banana leaf is a definite must-try.

Other tantalising treats include *otak otak*, a mildly spicy fish paste grilled inside a banana-leaf case held together by short skewers (these days, they may be stapled together – look out for the staples when you unwrap your *otak otak*), and satay.

MALAY STALLS

In most parts of Malaysia, you'll find stalls selling Malay hawker food grouped together. Similarly, in hawker centres and food courts in Singapore, most Malay food stalls are situated along the same stretch. Apart from *nasi lemak* (coconut rice with fried fish or other dishes) and *nasi campur*, they offer an extensive selection of halal dishes. These include *sop kambing* (mutton soup), *mee rebus* (thick egg noodles in a sweet and spicy sauce served with hard-boiled eggs and freshly cut green chillies), *mee siam* (*bee hoon* – rice vermicelli – in a spicy, tangy sauce), *mee soto* (thick egg noodles in broth, served with shredded chicken and bean sprouts), *tauhu goreng* (fried tofu topped with blanched bean sprouts, slivers of cucumber and a spicy-sweet peanut sauce) and halal chicken rice (the chicken is usually fried).

Often, you'll also find fried chicken wings coated in a deliciously spicy batter, *otak otak*, curry puffs (deep-fried pyramid-shaped pastries filled with spicy vegetable or meat curry), sardine puffs (tinned sardines in tomato sauce flaked and fried with shallots and chilli, then wrapped in pastry – a very tasty combination) and *kuih*, Malay cakes and sweets. Other Malay stalls sell only *nasi bubur* (rice porridge, also known as *congee*, served with side dishes).

DRINK STALLS

Easily identified by colourful displays of the different kinds of drinks they have on offer for the day, dedicated drink stalls are usually found in hawker centres, food courts and shopping malls. You may also come across them on busy street corners.

DESSERT STALLS

Malaysians and Singaporeans love desserts and sweet things. The varieties available are endless.

Chinese sweets tend to variations on syrupy soups: *tau suan* (split mung beans in a starchy, sweet soup), *cheng teng* (various nuts and dried fruit in a sweet syrup), *ah boling* (also spelled *ah balling*; glutinous rice-flour dumplings filled with black sesame paste, peanut paste, white sesame paste or red bean paste, served in a sweet peanut or ginger soup), *lek tau teng* (a sweet green-bean soup), *andang tau teng* (a sweet red-bean soup). Most of these desserts are served hot.

It's hard to resist the many different colourful *kuih* (cakes) displayed at Malay and Peranakan stalls. Choose from steamed *kuih lapis* (a cake with thin layers of different colours), *talam ubi* (a double-layered *kuih* with a coconut top layer and a lower layer made from sweet potato), *putri salat* (glutinous rice topped with a green, pandan leaf–infused custard), *bingke ubi* (a baked tapioca slice) and *kuih bakar* (pandan-flavoured custard cake) among other lovely options.

Indian sweets are truly only for the very sweet-toothed. They include *gulab jamun*, fried doughballs, made from milk solids, doused in syrup; slices of *palgoa*, made of cow's milk, *ghee* (clarified butter) and sugar; and *laddu*, made from yellow lentils, cow's milk and sugar.

Shaved ice desserts are also very popular. *Ais kacang* is a bowl of sweet red beans, corn kernels and multicoloured cubes of jelly, covered with a mountain of shaved ice and drizzled with condensed milk and coloured syrups.

It's rarer to come across the *ais ball*. Similar to the *ais kacang* in concept, the difference is that you can take an *ais ball* with you and eat it as you walk. Filled with a mixture of beans, the shaved ice is shaped by hand into a large ball and covered with rose syrup, condensed milk and *gula melaka* (palm sugar) syrup. It's presented to you in a plastic sheet and the challenge is for you to eat it all before the heat reduces it to a mushy slush!

ICE-CREAM FLAVOURS

Ice-cream trucks are little iceboxes on wheels, usually propelled by a bicycle attached to their frame. Listen out for the tinkle of a bell, indicating that the ice-cream truck is in the neighbourhood. Forget chocolate, vanilla and strawberry, the flavours to taste in Malaysia and Singapore are durian, coconut, sweetcorn and sour plum. While ice-cream cones are common, the traditional way to eat ice cream is to wedge a slice between two rectangular sheets of wafer, or between a folded slice of white bread like a sandwich.

From top: Fruit to go;
Ice cream served the
traditional Malay way

FRUIT STALLS

You can't miss them. They have wedges of ready-cut fruit in their display cases – anything from local *cikus* (sapodilla), guavas, *jambus* (wax apple) and rambutans to watermelons, apples and honeydew melons. Pick what you want, and the stallholder is likely to slice them and place them all on a dish for you. Guava is often served with sweet-and-sour plum powder and *jambu* with dark soy sauce and chilli. But the truly adventurous should look out for durian stalls that set up tables along the street. Pick your durian, have it opened for you, then just sit down and dig right in.

SNACK STALLS

Snack stalls are everywhere. You'll find roasted chestnuts, salted or sugared *kacang* (peanuts, dried peas and beans), *you char kway* (deep-fried dough sticks that are often served sliced in *rojak* or rice porridge and sometimes dipped into soya-bean milk), *keropok* (deep-fried fish crackers), *goreng pisang* (banana slices, deep-fried in a batter), pan-fried tapioca pancakes, *vadai* (savoury deep-fried Indian snacks), *pong piah* (also known as *roti timbu*; baked buns filled with yellow-bean paste, a Penang speciality), and even corn-on-the-cob slathered with margarine! In fact, a snack is basically anything locals feel like eating between meals. It could even be a small dish of vegetarian fried *bee hoon*, a *rojak*, or a pork-filled *pau* (a steamed bun).

KEDAI KOPI & KOPITIAM

These old-school coffeeshops serve as a meeting place where customers may stop for a *kopi* (coffee) or *teh* (tea), a snack or a fuller meal. They usually occupy the ground-level of shophouses – the combined residential and business spaces that are common across the region.

KOPITIAM EATS

Kedai kopi (the Malay term) and *kopitiam* (the more common Chinese term) usually open throughout the day. Don't expect air-conditioning or fancy table-side service. They are often set up like mini hawker centres, where you order from individuals stalls within the *kopitiam* that specialise in specific dishes. The variety is similar. You may find the *char kway teow* vendor, Indian *mee goreng* stall and *nasi lemak* counter. Each coffeeshop has its own unique mix of stalls. Some are exclusively Indian Muslim or Muslim. The best way for you to tell what kind of joint it is is to take a walk around inside. You're not obliged to stay and have a meal simply because you've taken a look around. The only constant is the drinks stall, which is usually owned by the person who also owns the property.

At a good number of coffeeshops, you'll discover that the hawkers working in the morning may be serving quite different things to their counterparts at night. They may share the same counter space, but one hawker serves his or her speciality in the morning, while the other does so at night (they split the rent, reducing their running costs). You could conceivably go to the same coffeeshop at different times of the day and have quite different meal choices presented to you. Walk up to the stall you wish to patronise, place your order, indicate which table you're seated at, then return to your seat and wait.

KOPITIAM DRINKS

The drink-stall vendor will usually come up to your table to ask you for your drink request. Most international brands of soft drinks will be available, in addition to local specialities such as soya-bean milk, *air cincau* (a sweet, dark-coloured drink filled with strings of black jelly), barley water or sweet chrysanthemum tea. But you won't find the drinks homemade in large vats the way you get them at hawker centres. Chinese or non-Muslim run *kopitiam* will also serve local *bir* (beer) such as Tiger and Anchor. But what locals usually come for is the local thick coffee and tea, sweetened with condensed milk. Don't be surprised if some of the older folks around you pour a portion of their coffee or tea into their saucers and sip out of them! This is a favoured method for quickly cooling down a piping-hot drink.

Opposite: KL's Yong Bee *kopitiam* is famous for its toast and *nasi lemak*
Left: *Kopi* served in a traditional cup and saucer

BAK KUT TEH

You may come across some *kopi-tiam* specialising in *bak kut teh* (literally 'pork bone tea' in Hokkien, although it contains no tea). This peppery pork soup filled with short lengths of pork rib, tender flesh just falling away from the bone, is served to you in bowls. And once you've downed all your soup (usually served with a bowl of plain white rice), you are often welcome to ask for a top-up of broth at no extra charge. The pork flesh, while not the focus of the meal, tastes lovely when dipped in soy sauce that has been infused with chopped red chillies. On the table will be large kettles of boiling water – this is for making the Chinese tea that you usually have along with this dish. The teapot and cups are doused in hot water (to ensure that they are clean and warm) before the packet of tea leaves is emptied into the pot. Allow the tea to brew for a few minutes – it should look fairly weak – before you pour it out into the Chinese teacups.

ROTI KAYA

A classic breakfast that is served in many *kopitiam* is *roti kaya*. *Roti* is Malay for bread and *kaya* is a sweet spread made from eggs, coconut milk, pandan leaf and sugar. Two slices of white bread are toasted and made into a sandwich with a filling of *kaya* and thick slices of ice-cold butter. You can also order a side dish of very soft-boiled eggs, which are cracked into a saucer and mixed with a splash of dark soy sauce and sprinkle of pepper. Either slurp this mixture down (it's quite acceptable to drink it from the lip of your saucer) or use it as a dip for your *roti kaya*. It's a tasty combination that is best washed down with a good cup of *kopi* or *teh*.

From left: *Bak kut teh; Roti kaya; Colourful dim sum*

DIM SUM

Some old-school Chinese *kopitiam* serve a short selection of dim sum for breakfast. Some places still use the pushcart steamers that are brought right to your table. Choose from *siu mai* (minced-pork dumplings); *har kow* (prawn dumplings); *fong zhao* (braised chicken feet), which the Cantonese prefer to call phoenix claws; *pai quat* (steamed pork ribs, usually with salted black beans); and a plethora of other steamed and fried delicacies. Don't expect to get as wide a selection of items as in dedicated dim sum restaurants. Remember that these are small establishments that often have tiny kitchens. They keep their menus pretty simple, offering just the classic crowd-pleasers. Ordering is a simple matter of pointing at what you want. The meals are usually accompanied by cups of Chinese tea.

TZE CHAR STALLS

One more type of *kopitiam* you may come across, particularly in Singapore, are ones with a *tze char* stall. This is the closest you get to a restaurant experience in a hawker context (you order everything from the one place). Identify these stalls by the whole uncooked fish hanging in the prominent chiller display and possibly bunches of fresh vegetables laid out in front.

They serve anything from *yu pian tang* (fish-slice soup), *har cheong kai* (chicken deep-fried in a prawn-paste batter) and *sa po taufu* (claypot tofu), to *kangkong sambal belacan* (water spinach stir-fried in a seafood sauce), *hor fun* (rice-based noodles in a thick broth with seafood and pork) and *ou nee* (a yam-paste dessert). Some will even serve steamed, chilli or pepper crab. Chances are, the *tze char* stall will have menus. But another strategy is to take a look at what others are eating and try to point them out to the person who's taking your order.

RESTAURANTS

A restaurant in Malaysia and Singapore covers a broad range of options. At one end are no-frills joints with no air-conditioning, surly service and decidedly local items on the menu. At the other are temples to fine dining with Michelin stars and cutting-edge gastronomy.

MAKANAN LAUT (SEAFOOD)

A prime example of the casual, no-frills restaurant is the *makanan laut restoran* (seafood restaurant). These are often found on or near the beach or coastline, sometimes with tables in the open – the kitchen is usually a permanent structure, while the seating area might not be. Otherwise, they are housed in airy buildings cooled by huge electric fans. These restaurants are beloved by both locals for communal meals and by tourists for their affordable seafood cooked the local way.

On the menu, you will find the fresh catch of the day, perhaps steamed *kerapu* (red grouper) or deep-fried *ikan merah* (red snapper). There might also be *kerang* (cockles) topped with chilli; *sambal kepah* (clams cooked in a chilli paste); steamed *gong gong* (sea snails served with a chilli dip); steamed *ketam renjong* (blue swimmer crab) served cold, Teochew style; or *ketam batu* (mud crab) cooked in a variety of curries, the most popular being simply known as chilli crab. Other cooked dishes may include *ngoh hiang*, also known as *lor bak* (deep-fried spring rolls containing a mixture of minced pork and prawn or fish); *you char kway* (deep-fried dough sticks) stuffed with seafood paste; *sambal kangkong* (water spinach stir-fried in a chilli paste); and seafood *hor fun* (stir-fried rice noodles with squid, prawns and other bits of seafood). Some

LOCAL FAST FOOD

Given the preponderance and popularity of hawker food in Malaysia and Singapore you'd wonder how international fast-food chains would ever stand a chance. Still, Malaysians and Singaporeans love a Big Mac or Nando's spicy chicken just as much as everyone else and you won't struggle to find any of your fast-food favourites. What makes these local franchises most interesting to overseas visitors is the chance to sample items specially developed for the local market. For example, in McDonald's look out for nasi lemak burgers and green tea or durian McFlurrys.

restaurants also offer *otak otak* (spiced rectangles of *tenggiri batang* – Spanish mackerel – wrapped in banana leaves and grilled over a charcoal fire), *rojak* and satay.

OLD-STYLE RESTAURANTS

Increasingly rare in the big cities, but more common in smaller Malaysian towns, are restaurants built or set up in the '60s and '70s. This is where you're mostly likely to find restaurants serving local cuisine – Peranakan, Malay, Chinese, sometimes Eurasian and Indian. The restaurants are low on ambience, but can serve good, local food at reasonable prices.

Falling into this category are restaurants originally set up by Hainanese cooks. Compared to the other Chinese regional groups, the Hainanese were among the last migrants to arrive in Malaysia and Singapore. This led to them taking up jobs as cooks and waiters in British and Peranakan households. Later, when these cooks struck out on their own, with old-school restaurants such as the Coliseum Cafe and Yut Kee in Kuala Lumpur, they chose to serve hybrid renditions of British and Peranakan cuisine, such as chicken chop or oxtail soup, as well as their own classic dishes like Hainanese chicken rice.

FORMAL RESTAURANTS

In the larger cities, you'll find formal restaurants serving traditional cuisine – more so for Chinese and Indian rather than Malay food, as Malays tend to prefer home cooking for special or formal occasions. These can be fancy joints with expensive menus and (for non-Muslim establishments) impressive wine lists.

The Chinese restaurants tend to be region-specific, choosing to serve either Cantonese (most common), Teochew or Hokkien specialities. But in Kuala Lumpur and Singapore you may also find

FORMAL MALAY eateries are VERITABLE HOMAGES to the intricacies of MALAY CUISINE and culture

Shanghainese, Hakka and Hockchew foods among the cuisines of other minority dialect groups.

There tend to be more restaurants specialising in North Indian cuisine than South Indian food. But at many Indian restaurants you can order from a menu that covers the most popular dishes from across the subcontinent.

Some of the Malay restaurants that do exist cater, to some extent, to a tourist crowd, and may feature cultural shows as part of the package. But the handful of truly formal Malay eateries are veritable homages to the intricacies of Malay cuisine and culture. What you will also find, particularly in Kuala Lumpur, George Town, Melaka and Singapore, are restaurants dedicated to Peranakan (or Nonya) cuisine.

VEGETARIAN & VEGAN DINING

The Chinese and Indians have venerable vegetarian traditions, and you should have no problem tracking down vegetarian and vegan food in the region's big cities. Once out in the countryside, though, be sure to check with the cook.

Hindu prohibitions against meat mean that the Little Indias of Kuala Lumpur, Singapore and George Town are fantastically well served with places serving vegetarian and vegan dishes. Look out for South Indian rice-flour treats such as *dosa* and *idli*. In North Indian restaurants, staples like *daal* (curried lentils), *paneer* (a type of cheese), and *naan* (bread) can all make up a veg meal. Vegans will have to watch out for the addition of eggs and milk in some Indian vegetarian cuisine but, on the whole, Indian is the easiest way to go.

Chinese stalls usually make their soup stock with animal bones. Cooks can also slip small quantities of pork (minced or ground) or lard into all sorts of dishes. It always pays to double check with the cook on this before ordering. In cities with sizeable Chinese populations you'll also likely find restaurants dedicated to Buddhist vegetarian cuisine. One local practice is for Chinese vegetarian restaurants to pack their menus with mock meat dishes made from various processed soya-bean products such as tofu and tempeh.

Malay food stalls and restaurants are the ones where you may have the most problems as many dishes are flavoured with *belacan* (fermented shrimp paste) or, like the coconut rice dish *nasi lemak*, come sprinkled with *ikan bilis* (fried anchovies). The vegetarian version of *nasi lemak* will have fried peanuts, cucumber, spicy tomatoes and chilli *sambal* served with the rice. *Popiah* spring rolls, as long as they're prepared without the addition of Chinese sausage or other meats, are also a great vegetarian option.

Be aware that interpretations of 'vegetarian' food can vary. Something labelled 'vegetable soup' on a menu can contain both chicken and prawn, the reasoning being that because it contains vegetables, it's a vegetable soup. Be highly specific when ordering – don't just say 'vegetarian', but stress that you eat 'no meat, no seafood'.

USEFUL PHRASES

Saya hanya makan sayuran
I only eat vegetables

Saya tidak makan produk haiwan
I don't eat animal products

Saya tidak makan yang di perbuat dari sayur, telur, ikan atau daging
I don't eat dairy products, eggs, fish or meat

Adakah anda mempunyai susu soya
Do you have soya milk?

HEALTHY EATING

For the most part, the food and water are safe to consume. However, the tropical and wet climate is a breeding ground for bacteria, so it pays to be careful. There are also some local remedies if you do end up getting sick.

HYGIENE

In Malaysia and Singapore all eateries are legally required to display their hygiene rating (issued by a governing body) in a prominent spot so that customers can decide whether or not they want to dine there. An A denotes the highest grading, while C denotes the lowest. If an eatery is given a D rating it gets shut down. However, whatever the rating, go with your gut. If the food looks unappetising and the hygiene of the stall and/or the cooks looks like it could be improved, it's probably not worth the risk, no matter how many locals are eating there.

WATER

Tap water in both Singapore and Malaysia is treated and is considered safe to drink in major towns and cities. But be sure to have your water boiled if you're out in a kampong (village) or undeveloped area. If you're not convinced of the cleanliness of city tap water, or feel your body is unaccustomed to the local water, you'll find bottled water is widely and cheaply available. As temperatures can soar during the day, you should carry a bottle of water with you, sipping often to keep yourself hydrated.

HEATINESS & COOLNESS

Traditional Chinese medicine believes in the concepts of 'heatiness' and 'coolness' as the body's primary forces. The idea is to maintain a balance between the two. When you hear someone saying that they're feeling heaty, chances are they're feeling the onset of a dry sore throat and have been overindulging in heaty foods such as chilli, fried fish or durian. Or they may be feeling cold, having eaten or drunk too many cooling foods and drinks such as green tea, cucumber and seafood. The trick is to consume more cooling foods if you're feeling heaty, or conversely increase your consumption of heaty foods if your body is too cool.

Chinese herbal tea stalls are common across the region. Ask the stallholder for advice; he or she should be able to recommend a tea to suit your needs. Otherwise, readily available drinks such as barley water, chrysanthemum tea, coconut water and *air cincau* (a dark-coloured drink filled with black strings of jelly) are considered cooling. *Ang cho* (dried red date) and longan teas are heaty. Beware of over-consumption, though. If your body is already cool, too much cooling tea in addition to cooling foods can give you the runs. Similarly, too much heaty food coupled with heaty teas can give you constipation.

& DRINKING

DIARRHOEA

Simple things like a change of water, food or climate can all cause a mild bout of diarrhoea, but a few rushed toilet trips with no other symptoms is not indicative of a major problem. However, if you're also suffering a high fever or passing blood, for example, consult a doctor immediately.

Dehydration is the main danger with any diarrhoea. Under all circumstances fluid replacement (at least equal to the volume being lost) is the most important thing to remember. Check your urine to assess how much liquid replenishment you need: small amounts of dark urine mean you should increase your intake by drinking small amounts regularly. Good sources of fluid are water and carbonated drinks left to go flat and mixed with an equal amount of clean water. If diarrhoea is severe, you may need to replace minerals and salts. There are a range of oral rehydration salts available – for a DIY version, take 1L (2 pints) of water and mix into it half a teaspoon of salt and six teaspoons of sugar.

Be aware that anti-diarrhoeal drugs don't actually cure the problem, they just slow the plumbing down so you don't have to visit the loo so often. These drugs can be helpful if you're ill and have to make a long journey; otherwise, let things run their course.

LOCAL REMEDIES

Generations of Chinese have been turning to Po Chai pills when they are experiencing diarrhoea or other gastrointestinal ailments. These can be picked up at any neighbourhood Chinese medicinal hall. For loose bowels, the Portuguese-Eurasian community turns to thick, hot tea. These folks swear by the two-teabags-in-half-a-teacup-of-water remedy when having 'the runs'. And if your issue is with flatulence, many locals swear that drinking *teh halia* (milky ginger tea) served at many tea stalls will rid you of the problem.

CONSTIPATION RELIEF

If you find yourself constipated, head to a fresh fruit stall and load up on papayas. These fruit with the bright orange flesh were once used to tenderise meat and serve as a superb natural substitute for chemist-bought laxatives. Alternatively, a pack of prunes or a bottle of prune juice should help things along.

ALLERGIES & INTOLERANCES

If you have food allergies, carefully check the ingredients used in all dishes you order — the addition of, say, nuts or seafood may not always be apparent. Those with an intolerance to gluten should of course avoid soy sauce and wheat noodles.

ALLERGIES

If you are allergic to seafood, watch out for cockles, which go into some noodle dishes like laksa and *char kway teow*. *Belacan* (shrimp paste) is also used in many Malay, Peranakan and Chinese dishes. Some sauces like satay sauce and the dressing in *rojak* (salad with shrimp-paste-based dressing) contain nuts.

INTOLERANCES

If you are lactose intolerant, you're going to have to pass on milky drinks such as *kopi* and *teh tarik*. Many Malay dishes contain *santan* (coconut milk) but as this doesn't contain any lactose you will be free to indulge. If you're gluten intolerant, then aim for noodle dishes made with rice noodles rather than wheat. Soy and oyster sauces usually contain wheat.

MSG

Ten minutes after a delicious meal, you suddenly suffer from an insatiable thirst, your lips feel like they're swollen and dry, your mouth tastes yucky and you're kind of sleepy. You may have the beginnings of a migraine. If this happens to you, you may be having an adverse reaction to MSG (monosodium glutamate).

Many eateries in Malaysia and Singapore use MSG to enhance the flavour of their food. You can request for your meals to come without MSG, but not all places will be able to meet that request — especially hawker stalls since parts of the dishes they serve are usually pre-prepared.

How to get some quick relief? Down an ice-cold, sugary carbonated drink, or try a good dose of freshly squeezed orange juice. Also drink plenty of water to help flush the MSG from your system.

DIABETICS

Malaysians and Singaporeans like their sweets. Whether it's brightly coloured *ais kacang* or Indian *kulfi* (ice cream made with reduced milk and flavoured with a variation of nuts, fruits and berries) or Peranakan *pulut hitam* (sweet, sticky black-rice pudding), there's always a dessert stall offering local delights at any hawker centre. These desserts are practically impossible to resist, but do note (particularly if you're diabetic) that they have an immensely high sugar content.

FOREIGN FOOD

The national cuisines of Malaysia and Singapore are by their very nature multicultural. But, particularly in the major cities, you will also find no shortage of places offering regional Asian cuisines such as Thai, Japanese and Korean, as well as common Western foods such as burgers and pizza.

Japan's brutal colonisation of the Malay Archipelago and Singapore during WWII may have left some older citizens with bad memories, but that doesn't seem to have affected the way that everyone now laps up Japanese food. In Malaysia's larger cities and Singapore you won't have to go far to stumble across a restaurant or stall serving Japanese favourites such as sushi, ramen noodles and tempura. Some high-end places even fly in their ingredients – including fresh fish and seafood – direct from Japan each day.

Other types of Asian eateries are popular with locals, in particular those specialising in the food of near neighbours Thailand, Indonesia and Vietnam. In Kuala Lumpur and Singapore you may also come across places serving dishes from Myanmar, including the soup noodles *moun-hin-ga* or the fermented green-tea-leaf salad *laphet*. Up and coming in both cities are Korean restaurants serving delicious meals such as crispy chicken, cook-at-the-table barbecued beef and pork ribs, and the rice-salad dish *bibimbap*.

Both Kuala Lumpur and Singapore have thriving restaurant scenes that are fully plugged into international dining trends. In either city, take your pick from practically every other type of global cuisine, from authentic Italian pasta and pizza to tacos and enchiladas that would gain Mexican approval.

Talented chefs from around the globe now see KL and Singapore as places to establish or expand on their reputations, and the two cities foster great creativity in the kitchen. Whether it's modern Chinese cuisine or a subtle fusion of different cuisines (be it Japanese and French, Vietnamese and French or Hawaiian and Californian), the dining experiences open to you are unique, exciting and of an impressively high quality.

The 2019 Michelin dining guide to Singapore awarded 44 restaurants with stars for their culinary excellence. While some of them serve superb renditions of Chinese and Indian food, the coveted stars are mainly for restaurants specialising in either Japanese or various styles of European cuisine. The cutting-edge French restaurants Odette, helmed by Julien Royer, and Les Amis, where the exec chef is Sebastien Lepinoy, both gained the top grade of three stars.

WINES &
TAPAS served
here

STAPLES & SPECIALITIES

Left: Spicy, tangy and delicious Peranakan curry laksa

M alaysian and Singaporean pantries are mixed bags of tricks filled with spices, herbs, grains, sauces and many other ingredients from a host of cuisines, each continually borrowing from the other. Rather than attempt to redraw those lines, local chefs celebrate in the blurring of boundaries, creating distinctive local dishes that play with the rich food choices open to them.

Rice (*nasi* in Malay) is at the heart of Malaysian and Singaporean cuisine, a defining feature of their many food cultures. It's eaten daily, either as cooked rice or indirectly in the form of rice flour in dishes ranging from a breakfast bowl of *congee* (rice porridge) to laksa rice noodles and *kuih* (cakes).

With a lengthy coastline and many islands, rivers and lakes it's no surprise that fish and seafood are also staple sources of protein in both countries. Malaysians are among the world's biggest consumers of fish, eating at least 56.5kg (125lb) of fish per person each year. Even when a dish might not seem to have fish in it, it may well be flavoured with a pinch of *belacan*, the pungent paste made from salted, fermented shrimp that is a common ingredient in Malaysian cooking.

Other popular proteins are chicken, duck, beef and mutton, with pork a winner among non-Muslims. Herbs and vegetables also play a starring role, with vegetables in one form or another featuring in most meals, from the slices of cucumber served with the coconut-rice dish *nasi lemak* to the *petai* (stink beans) in stir-fries and curries. And a bewildering range of tropical fruit is eaten as snacks or dessert or made into juice.

Left: Grains of rice in the field

When cooked it's extremely sticky and is easily moulded into shapes. Malays use the white variety of this rice in *lemang*, a sticky-rice dish originating in Negeri Sembilan that is shaped into tubes in the hollow of long bamboo poles. Peranakans (and Malays) also use it in rice-based desserts such as *kuih putri salat*, a double-layered cake consisting of a glutinous rice base covered with a thick, sweet, green-coloured (derived from the pandan leaf), custard-like topping. Made in large slabs, the cake is sliced into tiles of green and white.

RiCE

The average Malaysian eats around 80kg (176lb) of rice per year. Local production meets approximately 65% of domestic demand, with the balance imported from neighbouring Southeast Asian countries. The northern states of Kedah and Perlis, which produce most of the country's crop, are often referred to as the rice bowl of Malaysia. Singaporeans eat more than 300

bowls of rice a year, which requires the annual import of around 300,000 tons of the grain.

Among Indians, basmati rice (translated literally from Hindi as 'fragrant') is preferred for special occasions and particular dishes. The grains should be white, long and silky to the touch; good basmati is supposed to be left to mature for up to 10 years. When cooked, it has a unique fragrance and distinct nutty flavour. Basmati can be served mixed with nuts and spices and infused with the wonderful flavour of *ghee* (clarified butter).

Glutinous rice is either white or black in colour and comes in short- and long-grain varieties.

WAYS OF COOKING

These days many Malaysian and Singaporean households will own a rice cooker. But the time-honoured way to prepare plain, steamed rice is in a pot of boiling water. This absorption method of cooking rice involves bringing water to the boil, and then adding washed, drained rice grains into it. By the time the rice is cooked tender, it will have absorbed all the water, giving it the perfect consistency. The general ratio is one cup of long-grain rice to two cups of water, but the age and variety of the grain affects the amount of water you need to use. For example, you need less water for short-grain rice.

Types of Rice

The most popular types of rice in Malaysia and Singapore are as follows:

LOCAL WHITE RICE

This paddy-grown variety is a medium-length, white kernel that stays firm after cooking and has no distinct aroma. It can be used in a variety of recipes and suits the multicultural Malaysian palate.

IMPORTED WHITE RICE

White rice imported from both Thailand and Vietnam is popular in Malaysia. The grains are of medium-size, but Vietnamese rice is slightly shorter and wider compared to its Thai counterpart.

BROWN RICE

Also known as 'hulled' or 'unmilled' rice, it has a mild, nutty flavour and is chewier than the white varieties. It's used for making fried rice and can can also be served plain with side dishes.

JASMINE RICE

Imported from Thailand and prized for its aroma and flavour. Purists recommend against serving curry with jasmine rice, because this fragrant variety works against the flavour of the curry.

BASMATI RICE

A long, slender and aromatic rice imported from India or Pakistan. This creamy white rice doubles in size when cooked and is a perfect choice for biryanis.

PONNI RICE

This easy to prepare, Indian-origin rice has a shorter, plump, almost round kernel. The cooked grains have a slight springiness to the bite. It's typically served alongside spicy Indian curries.

GLUTINOUS RICE

Also known as sticky, waxy and sweet rice. It is usually served as an accompaniment to fried salted fish and grated coconut, or prepared sweet topped with coconut cream and fresh-cut mangoes.

JAPONICA RICE

Although the short, plump grains still separate when cooked, this rice is moist and tender and has a slightly sticky texture. It is used for sushi and other Japanese dishes

From top: Hawker preparing *nasi lemak; Nasi lemak* ready to eat

NASi LEMAK

A very common way for a Malaysian to start their day is with a breakfast of *nasi lemak*. Literally meaning 'fatty rice', *nasi lemak* gets its name from the cooking process of the rice which makes the grain rich, creamy and fragrant in taste and mouthfeel. It is so beloved in Malaysia that creative chefs and major fast-food chains have brought out their own spin on the original, with *nasi lemak* burgers, cake and even ice cream.

In its original form this dish consists of lightly salted rice, cooked with coconut milk and a flavouring of pandan leaves, topped with chilli *sambal*, *ikan bilis* (fried dried anchovies) and a few slices of cucumber, all wrapped up in a banana leaf. You'll find these neat little packages for sale at makeshift stalls near bus interchanges and busy thoroughfares.

If you're eating the dish in a *kopitiam* or restaurant then it is also typically served on a plate with additional sides of toasted peanuts and halves of a boiled egg. What really makes the dish is the spicy quality of the *sambal*, which helps bring all the other milder flavours together.

Some *nasi lemak* stalls offer a wider selection of items for customers to add to the basic dish, such as fried chicken, beef *rendang* (beef in a thick coconut-milk curry sauce), fried egg or deep-fried fish. Instead of just coconut rice, they may also offer *nasi kuning* (rice turned yellow with the addition of turmeric).

Sometimes at *nasi lemak* stalls, a banana-leaf-shaped into a cone is filled with your choice of rice before adding meat, fish or vegetable items as required on top. There will be long queues at the best *nasi lemak* stalls, and although it is a common breakfast dish, it's also served and enjoyed as a meal at any time of day.

THE SiNGAPOREAN VERSiON

The nasi lemak you may come across in Singapore can have some differences from its Malaysian counterpart. The rice may be dyed green from pandan-leaf essence or extract. The sambal may be sweeter and less spicy so as not to overpower the more delicate flavours of the other elements of the meal. The dish may be served with an omelette or fried egg rather than boiled egg. And in the island's Chinese-run kopitiam, a fried slice of the pork luncheon meat Spam – haram (forbidden) to Muslims – may be available.

RiCE MEALS

Rice is the centrepiece of many types of meal in Malaysia and Singapore. It's front and centre at Malay *nasi campur* and Chinese economy-rice stalls as well as present in Indian biryani and banana-leaf rice eateries.

The concept of picking items to go with a basic portion of rice is also found at *nasi campur, nasi padang, nasi kandar, chap chye peng* (economy rice) and banana-leaf rice restaurants and stalls. The customer starts with a plate of rice and identifies what other cooked dishes, from the array on display, he or she wishes to add to the rice. As the name implies, banana-leaf rice restaurants serve the grain on a fresh, glossy and mildly fragrant banana leaf.

You may get a choice of plain white rice, coconut rice and yellow rice at all the different kinds of stalls, except at the economy-rice stall where only plain white rice is served. *Nasi campur* is the Malay version, while the very similar *nasi padang* originates from Indonesia. *Nasi kandar*, made famous in Penang, is the Indian version. Economy rice is the Chinese interpretation of the same concept. Essentially, the kind of dishes sold at each type of stall reflects its cuisine traditions. However, such distinctions are not set in stone, and you are likely to find an Indonesian-style *rendang* at the *nasi campur* stall or chicken curry at the economy-rice stall.

© szefei | Getty Images

Left: The blue colour of *nasi kerabu* comes from the butterfly pea flower

NASI BIRYANI

A biryani is a rich, aromatic rice casserole often layered with meat (most often chicken or mutton) then steamed gently so that the flavours blend. While it is a dish quite commonly found at Indian and Malay coffeeshops and stalls, the good stuff is only to be had at weddings and other special occasions where it is cooked at home. The trick is to follow the traditional Indian technique of frying the dish's dry spices in oil until aromatic, then browning the onions, tossing the uncooked rice grains into the mixture and coating the grains with the oil before cooking them. The best biryanis are flavoursome all the way through, while the meat remains tender and moist.

KETUPAT & LEM

KETUPAT

Ketupat is made in small cases woven from pliable strips of young, green coconut-palm leaves. They are filled up to the halfway mark with washed, uncooked rice before they are sealed. The cases are tied together in bundles and lowered into a pot of boiling water where they are left to simmer for four hours. To serve, the cooled rice packages are split in half lengthwise and the two halves of rice then cut into cubes (you get anywhere from eight to 18 cubes from a *ketupat* case).

This rice is commonly eaten with satay or curry. You are most likely to come across *ketupat* at satay stalls where they may be brought to the table still sitting in their split-open palm-leaf cases. Spear a cube of the pressed rice cake with a satay stick, add a slice of the accompanying onion or pineapple, then dip it into the thick and spicy peanut sauce.

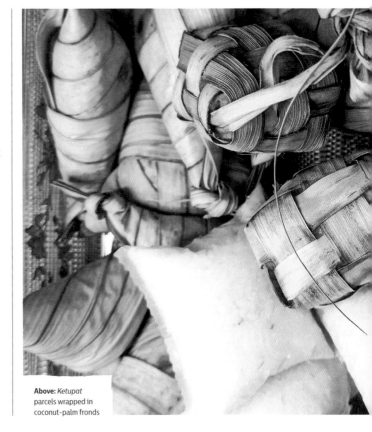

Above: *Ketupat* parcels wrapped in coconut-palm fronds

Right: *Lemang* cooking in bamboo poles

ANG

LEMANG

This speciality from Negeri Sembilan calls for bamboo poles cut into roughly 40cm (16in) lengths. Each is lined with banana leaf before it is filled with pre-soaked glutinous rice and coconut milk. The poles are lined up over a charcoal fire and left to cook for around four hours. When done, the banana-leaf package is extracted by splitting the bamboo. The cooked rice is then removed from the leaf and sliced into short, cylindrical portions. Not easy to find at restaurants or hawker stalls, you're more likely to find roadside stalls out in the suburbs or country selling *lemang* to women who serve it to their families at home. The delicate coconut flavour and aroma and moist sticky consistency of *lemang* offer a gastronomic experience not to be missed.

KETUPAT PULUT

In Malaysia's Kedah state, ketupat pulut *seems to bring elements of* ketupat *and* lemang *together. Glutinous rice is half-cooked in coconut milk before it is rolled into thick logs and wrapped in banana leaves. The logs are then steamed before they are unwrapped and served in cylindrical slices with* serunding daging *(a spicy beef floss; beef cooked to the point where it is dry and flaky, so it breaks down into a coarse, thread-like consistency).*

© Nadmin | Shutterstock; Everything You Need | Shutterstock

97

CONGEE/BUBUR

This rice-porridge dish is known as *congee* or *bubur* depending on which ethnic community Malaysians and Singaporeans hail from. It's often eaten for breakfast, or as a comfort food, particularly by the sick, and has both savoury and sweet recipes.

CHINESE VERSIONS

Congee, or rice porridge, is a Chinese dish in origin. However, it is prepared slightly differently and known by different names in different parts of China, hence affecting what the dish is called by the Chinese communities of Malaysia and Singapore.

To the Teochews it's *muay*, a plain rice porridge flavoured with just a hint of salt, served in place of steamed rice. Teochews like the rice grains to remain whole, so that the porridge really looks like rice in soup. They serve it with a selection of pickles, omelettes, braised and stewed meat dishes, fish and tofu. The Teochew version is a favourite supper dish in Singapore.

The Cantonese call the dish *chok* or *jok*. They prefer it served as a smooth porridge with the rice grains broken down to an almost pasty consistency. Extra ingredients are then added – classic

combinations include century egg (preserved egg) and minced pork, shredded chicken, or delicate slices of fish. You will often find these available in restaurants serving dim sum, or at Chinese coffeeshops.

The Hakkas have a very traditional dish that goes by the strange name *lui char fan* (thunder-tea rice). *Lui* is the Hakka word for grinding, but it also means

thunder. Traditionally, a pestle made from guava wood is used to grind ingredients such as peanuts, sesame seeds, peppercorns, Chinese tea leaves, mint leaves and sweet potato leaves in a large bowl. They are then steeped in hot water, poured into a pan and brought to a boil. The resulting soup is then poured over cooked rice, turning it into porridge.

98

Left: *Nasi bubur* with all the trimmings.
Right, from top: *Congee* with century egg and oyster; *Bubur hitam*; *You char kway* (fried dough sticks)

MALAY VERSIONS

For Malays rice porridge is called *bubur* and it's typically a dish made and enjoyed at home. *Bubur lambuk* (savoury rice porridge), for example, is flavoured with ginger, cinnamon, star anise and sometimes coconut, as well as coarsely chopped beef, diced chicken and diced prawns (yes, all three ingredients together). There's a tradition of eating *bubur lambuk* to break the fast during the month of Ramadan.

You will find some stalls – usually open at night – serving *nasi bubur*, an eastern Malaysian speciality. The texture is like that of Teochew porridge and, as with Teochew porridge, it's served with a variety of dishes you pick from a selection on display. But that's where the similarities stop. Accompanying dishes include fried stingray, fried quail, pickled garlic and cuttlefish with honey (which tastes almost candied). Salty, sweet and subtly spicy flavours dominate.

Bubur hitam, on the other hand, is a sweet porridge made of black glutinous rice, flavoured with *gula melaka* and pandan leaf and served with coconut milk.

NOODLES

Noodles were introduced into the Malay Archipelago from China. The two main types are *mian* or *mee* (made with wheat) and *mee fian* (made with rice). You may also find noodles made from other types of starch such as mung-bean flour.

LAN

If a restaurant or stall in Malaysia or Singapore is advertising itself as offering *lamian* it will be serving hand-made wheat-flour noodles. *Lamian* are also referred to as 'pulled' noodles, after the way the chef pulls out, or stretches, the dough to create the slender ropes that will eventually be cut into noodles. At some places you'll be able to watch the chef in action preparing the noodles. This more artisan-type of noodle may be served in soups with *wontons* (ravioli-like dumplings filled with meat, seafood or vegetables), or dry in *zha jiang mian* (literally 'fried sauce noodles'), a Beijing speciality made with a thick minced pork and ground-bean sauce.

MIAN XIAN

Also known as *misua* or *mee suah*, these slender, dried wheat-flour noodles are the Asian equivalent of Italian vermicelli. They are commonly found at hawker centres, served at Chinese stalls in a clear soup with pig's kidney or liver (and sometimes with a dash of brandy for good measure). Chinese eat the dish for its restorative qualities. Peranakans use the same noodles in *mee suah tow*, a stir-fry with shrimp, chicken and Chinese mushrooms. They call these 'birthday noodles'.

MEE

Mee – noodles made from a combination of wheat flour and eggs – are more common in Malaysia and Singapore than noodles made only from wheat flour. This fine, rounded egg noodle is somewhere between the thickness of angel hair pasta and spaghetti, and is the basic noodle served either dry and stir-fried, on in a soup along with or *char siew* (slices of barbecued pork)

MEE POK

When egg noodles are made flat, like linguini, they are called *mee pok*. You usually get to choose between these and regular *mee* when ordering most noodle dishes. But *mee pok* is preferred when having *bak chor mee* – noodles doused with Chinese black vinegar and the hawker's special sauce, then topped with minced pork, fish balls, pickles, freshly chopped spring onions and toasted dried fish.

HOKKIEN MEE

Hailing from China's Fujian province, these yellow, thick egg noodles are popular with all of Malaysia and Singapore's ethnic groups. They give their name to the dish *Hokkien mee,* the recipe for which will differ widely, depending on the location in which you order it.

If you're on the island of Penang, *Hokkien mee* is a prawn noodle soup. Both thick yellow *mee* and thin rice noodles are served together in a spicy broth in which dried prawns enhance the flavour. The noodle soup is usually topped with prawns, bean sprouts and fried onions with optional *sambal*. In Singapore this dish is sometimes known as *hae mee.*

Kuala Lumpur's style of *Hokkien mee* is broad yellow noodles mixed with slices of pork, squid and spring onion all stir-fried in a sweet, dark soy sauce. The Singapore variant again opts for stir-fried noodles but this time a mix of the thick yellow egg noodles and either thick or thin rice noodles with prawns, fish cake, squid and maybe egg.

KWAY TEOW

These broad ribbons of rice-flour noodle form the cornerstone of one of the region's much-loved Chinese hawker classics, *char kway teow* – stir-fried broad, flat rice-flour noodles tossed with cockles, slivers of Chinese sausage and egg in a sweet, dark soy sauce. Every local has a favourite stall. These noodles are also served in *yu yuan mian* (fish-ball soup).

LAKSA MEE

While you'll find as many different versions of laksa (a spicy, soupy noodle dish) as there are states in Malaysia, the noodles used remain fairly constant: white, opaque, thick rice-flour noodles similar in size to Hokkien noodles. Laksa is also served with Chinese beef noodles. Dried versions are also available, but the texture and flavour can be quite different to fresh versions.

Every LOCAL HAS A favourite STALL

From far left: A noodle hawker at Kimberley Street Night Market, George Town; *Char kway teow*

BEE HOON

Thin and brittle looking, these rice-flour noodles (also spelled *bihun*) have to be softened in water before they can be stir-fried or added to soups and curries. Simply stir-fried with dried shrimp, cabbage, carrot and perhaps some chicken, they form a casual lunchtime meal in most Malay and Chinese households. They can also be served in *mee siam*, a spicy and tangy Malay noodle dish influenced by the cuisine of neighbouring Thailand; and in Chinese hawker noodle dishes such as fish-ball soup.

TANG HOON

Also called glass noodles or cellophane noodles, *tang hoon* are usually made from mung bean flour. They look a little like *bee hoon* tied up in a bundle, but are difficult to cut or break in their dried state. They need to be soaked in water before stir-frying or boiling in soup. In most Chinese seafood restaurants, you are likely to find dishes such as claypot *tang hoon* with crab or prawns. At home, the noodles are also stir-fried with simple ingredients or popped into a soup.

INSTANT NOODLES

The variety of instant noodles available in Singapore and Malaysia is astounding. You will find both wheat- and rice-flour varieties at all supermarkets, with flavours created to appeal to local palates. A popular hawker dish is Maggi mee goreng, using Maggi brand instant noodles, softened in boiling water before being fried and topped with an egg fried sunny-side up. You'll often find this dish served at Indian Muslim stalls at suppertime.

RoTi

Wheat-based breads – *roti* in Malay – in Malaysia and Singapore's culinary scene are a legacy of the food preferences of British colonials and Indian migrants. From the Brits came the fluffy white loaf, slices of which are toasted for *roti kaya* (*kaya* being a sweet spread made from eggs, sugar, coconut milk and pandan leaf). But it's the Indian breads that are firm local favourites, such as pan-fried *roti canai*, also known as *roti prata* in Singapore and some parts of Malaysia.

Although its roots are with the southern Indian Tamils, *roti canai* (pronounced 'cha-nai') is a wholly local recipe; you'll be hard-pressed to find an exact equivalent of it elsewhere on the subcontinent. In its most basic form, *roti canai* is made from a low-protein wheat flour (like the plain all-purpose flour used for baking cakes), water, and oil or *ghee* (clarified butter). *Canai* is believed to come from the Malay word meaning to knead, which is a key part of the dough's preparation.

The dough is kneaded and left to rest three times. A ball of the rested dough is then slapped down against a well-oiled surface and stretched it out until it is thin and translucent. The most accomplished chefs will toss the dough in the air, like in the preparation of pizza, to make it stretch. Whatever method is used, the process is repeated several times before the dough is folded over on itself, into either a square or a round, capturing air bubbles between the layers. The flat-bread is then quickly fried on a griddle, until the outer layer is crispy, and the inside ones more moist and chewy. The classic *roti canai* is eaten freshly cooked, torn into small pieces to be dipped in a thin *daal* (lentil curry) and/or various other soupy curries such as *kari ayam* (with chicken) or *kari ikan* (with fish).

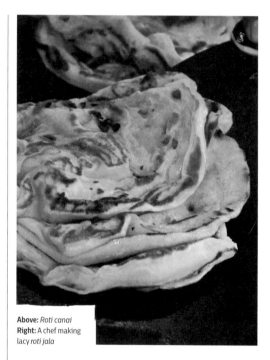

Above: *Roti canai*
Right: A chef making lacy *roti jala*

MURTABAK

A popular street food in Malaysia and Singapore, murtabak *is typically served at Indian Muslim food stalls known as* mamaks. *It's made using the same dough as* roti canai, *but not stretched out so thinly. It is then folded like a pancake or crêpe around savoury or sweet fillings before being griddle-fried.*

Know your Roti

At any stall serving *roti canai* you can usually order a host of variations to suit your palate. Among the popular options are:

ROTI BAWANG

Chopped onion (*bawang* in Malay) is sprinkled across the *roti* dough before it's folded and fried.

ROTI TELUR

A superb breakfast combo is having an egg (*telur*) cracked onto the dough before it's folded and fried.

ROTI CHEESE

Roti canai but with grated white cheese (usually a type of mozzarella) added before the dough is fried.

ROTI PLANTA

Thick smears of the popular Malaysian margarine brand, Planta, are added to the dough prior to cooking.

ROTI JALA

A batter of flour, milk and egg (perhaps with a pinch of turmeric for colour) is drizzled onto a griddle in a circular motion to create lacy pancakes. Rolled up, these can be dipped into curries.

ROTI TISU

The dough for this 'tissue bread' is spread out until it's paper thin, so as to create a very crispy texture. It's sometimes called *roti rocket* when served shaped into a cone.

ROTI SUSU

Sugar is the key addition to this 'sweet' *roti*. Eat it either with the normal curries for a sweet and salty combo or, if you have a really sweet tooth, dipped into condensed milk.

ROTI PISANG

Chopped *pisang* (banana) is added to the dough before frying for a naturally sweet *roti*. It's Malaysia and Singapore's take on a banana pancake.

DiM SUM

These steamed dumplings and buns, baked pastries and other small treats are a beloved facet of the local dining scene. There are hundreds of different dishes to choose from, which can either be enjoyed as snack or as a full meal.

For Malaysians and Singaporeans, gathering with family and friends for a Sunday brunch of dim sum is a regular event. There are even halal (pork-free) dim sum restaurants for Muslim Malays. The dishes are traditionally served with Chinese tea – hence yum cha, the other common name for them, which translates as 'drink tea'.

Dim sum are a Cantonese speciality, although you are likely to find other regional Chinese foods on the menu. They are also principally a breakfast and lunch food, served at dedicated restaurants and, in a smaller selection, at coffeeshops. Stalls at hawker centres may also sell them throughout the day and into the night. At the more traditional restaurants and coffeeshops, serving carts laden with bamboo steaming baskets and plates of the snacks are pushed around the dining area by waiters. Customers stop the waiter when they see something they'd like to try.

Dim sum include an assortment of seafood, meat and vegetable dishes that can be steamed, fried or baked. Popular ones include:

SHUMAI

Steamed dumplings, made from a thin dough wrapper shaped into a cup and filled with a mixture of minced pork and prawns, and chopped water chestnuts and bamboo shoots.

XIAOLONG BAO

Be careful not spill their hot, pork-broth contents when you chomp into these 'soup dumplings'. Originally from Shanghai, they are usually eaten dipped into black Chinese vinegar with slivers of ginger.

CHAR SIU BAO

Chunks of barbecued roast pork in a sweet sauce are embedded inside soft dough and steamed to make a soft, fluffy bun.

CHEONG FUN

Lasange-like sheets of rice-flour dough are wrapped around a prawn, pork or beef filling to create a soft roll that is lightly steamed and served dressed with soy sauce and sesame oil.

Right: Choices, choices: a selection of dim sum

HAR GOW

Diced prawns wrapped in a thin, translucent dough wrapper that is crimped into a half-moon bonnet shape, then steamed.

EGG TARTS

Puff pastry tartlets filled with a sweet egg custard. Other common sweet dim sum include sesame balls (balls of glutinous rice filled with sweet beans, covered with sesame seeds and deep-fried) and chilled mango pudding.

CHILLIES

Malaysians and Singaporeans love chilli. Even delicate dim sum is often served with a dish of chilli sauce on the side for that extra zing.

Red chilli adds colour and heat to a dish. Blended and ground with other spices, it adds depth to a curry. Sliced finely, it is tossed into anything from vegetable stir-fries to fried *bee hoon* and adds a punch to most dishes. Several chillies blended on their own form the base for many a *sambal* and chilli sauce.

Don't underestimate the importance of chilli sauce in a dish. A serving of chicken rice, for example, is not simply judged by the merits of the chicken, but also by the quality and flavour of the chilli sauce – which must contain a good balance of fresh red chillies, garlic, ginger and a hint of tartness from lime juice. Some places use commercial chilli pastes, others pride themselves in making their own.

REMPAH (SPICE PASTE)

While chilli paste is made up of large quantities of chilli blended into a paste – so as to sidestep the chore of grinding fresh chillies from scratch every time you make a dish – *rempah* is a mix of spices and aromatics created by pounding a combination of wet and dry ingredients together to form a paste. The recipe constantly changes depending on the dish you are making. Wet ingredients include shallots, lemongrass, garlic, chilli, ginger and galangal. Dry ingredients may be candlenuts, cinnamon, coriander seeds, cumin, cloves and peppercorns. Traditionally the ingredients are combined using a mortar and pestle, but a food processor is often used in the modern kitchen. The wet ingredients are combined before the dry ones are added.

Rempah is considered the heart and soul of Malay, Eurasian and Peranakan curries and sauces. It thickens curry gravies and gives dimension to their flavour, as

REMEDIES FOR CHILLI BURN

Milk provides a quick remedy for a tongue burning from too much chilli, but note that this combination can also have an upsetting effect on the stomach. Other popular remedies include eating a good mouthful of plain rice, or drinking warm water, iced water or calamansi juice.

curries flavoured with only curry powder tend to have a flat, bland taste. Beyond pounding it into a paste, the other important technique lies in frying *rempah*. A significant amount of oil is needed to fry the paste until it is fragrant. The oil has to be hot enough before the *rempah* is added to the pan. It must also be constantly stirred to prevent it from sticking. Once the oil starts to seep out of the *rempah*, the other ingredients in your recipe (say chicken for a chicken curry) can be added to the pan.

SAMBAL

There are as many kinds of *sambal* (basically a chilli sauce or relish) as there are cooks. At its most simple, the *sambal ulek* or *olek* is a combination of chilli, vinegar and salt blended either with a mortar and pestle or in a food processor. The basic chilli paste can be served on the side with a squirt of lime or calamansi juice as a condiment that will add a kick to your meal – you'll find it's served with anything from fried Hokkien noodles and laksa (a spicy, soupy noodle dish), to *nasi lemak* (coconut rice) and barbecued chicken wings. It can also be incorporated into curries and other spicy local dishes including barbecued fish and fried eggplant.

By adding shallots, galangal, garlic, *belacan*, tamarind liquid and other ingredients at hand, different kinds of *sambal* are created, all with the essential spicy punch at their core. Eurasians serve *sambal chilli taucheo* (onions, chilli and preserved soya beans) over fried fish or pan-fried *taukua* (firm bean curd) squares. Malays love their *nasi lemak* with *sambal ikan bilis*, in which the spicy chilli-based condiment is mixed with dried and fried anchovies. And Peranakans cannot bear to face a meal without a helping of *sambal belacan* (chilli and *belacan* paste) – diehard fans have been known to indulge in tiny helping of the *sambal* spread on toast.

TYPES OF CHILLI

CILI PADI (BIRD'S EYE CHILLI)

By far the spiciest of chillies. You'll know if you've bitten into this type of chilli as the heat will sear through your tongue and your eyes will start to water. They are sometimes served sliced and in soy sauce. Just a tiny hint of this chilli-soy sauce in your food will infuse it with a delightfully fiery heat.

LADA KERING (DRIED CHILLIES)

Next down in the heat scale. Dried chillies lack the strong aroma of fresh chillies, but often give dishes a brighter red colour. They need to be soaked in hot water until soft (usually just a few minutes) before they are used. In Sichuan cuisine, whole dried chillies are used in stir-fries. Malays believe that a few dried chillies should be put into a cook's rice bin to prevent weevils from attacking rice grains.

CHILLI OIL

Made using a base oil such as a vegetable oil, which is then infused with chilli. To make your own, simply heat one cup of oil in a small pan and stir in 10 whole dried chillies. Heat for one minute, then turn off the heat and leave to cool before straining. Use chilli oil sparingly as it has quite a spicy heat. It is usually used as a condiment rather than as part of a dish – you'll find little bottles of chilli oil at stalls serving *hay mee* (the Penang style of Hokkien prawn noodle soup).

GREEN CHILLIES

Less spicy than their red counterparts, green chillies impart a subtle flavour. At Chinese noodle hawkers, pickled cut green chillies are often served with light soy sauce as a dip to accompany light, soupy noodle dishes such as fish-ball noodles or *hor fun* (thick rice-based noodles cooked in a thick broth with seafood and pork).

Clockwise from top left:
Smoked catfish; *Ikan bilis*
(anchovies); Fresh stingrays
at the market; Stingray
asam curry

FISH &

With over **5000km (3100 miles)** of coastline between them it's hardly surprising that fish features heavily in the cuisine of Malaysia and Singapore. Explore any wet market and you'll find the variety of fresh fish and seafood that's available is mind-boggling.

Ikan (fish)

Malays generally prefer their fish fried whole and stuffed with spices or chopped into chunks or steaks and served in a spicy *asam* (tamarind) sauce. Chinese prefer to cook larger fish such as sea bass, grouper and snapper either steamed (when the fish is extremely fresh), fried or braised.

WOLF HERRING
(Ikan Parang)
Also known as *sai dou* in Cantonese, this silvery-scaled marine fish

is a key ingredient in the Johor version of laksa (a spicy, soupy noodle dish).

SPANISH MACKEREL
(Ikan Tenggiri)
Used in the Penang version of laksa as well as in fish curries. Minced and blended into a smooth paste with spices and flavourings including lemongrass, galangal and coconut, it is part of the recipe for *otak otak*.

ANCHOVIES
(Ikan Bilis)
Tiny anchovies spoil easily and are only sold fresh in the immediate vicinity of where they're caught/fished. You are most likely to find them salted or dried. Deep-fried, they are a traditional topping to the breakfast rice dish *nasi lemak*.

STINGRAY
(Ikan Pari)
Grilled stingray, or *ikan pari bakar* as it is known locally, is a very popular dish. The fish is marinated with chilli paste and herbs before being wrapped in banana leaves. It is then grilled over charcoal and eaten with a spicy, tangy dip.

CATFISH
(Ikan Patin)
This large freshwater fish, a speciality of Pahang, is cooked in various ways such as *gulai* (in a curry sauce) or in *asam pedas* (a sour sauce).

SEAFOOD

SEAFOOD

Clockwise from top left: Singapore chilli crab; Stuffed squid; Wok-fred cockles

Crabs
(Ketam)
For that special meal, Singapore chilli crab (stir-fried in a spicy chilli and tomato sauce), black pepper crab (stir-fried in a sweet and spicy chilli and black pepper sauce), or simple steamed crab are much-loved treats. All are made with mud crab.

Cockles
(Kerang)
These small shellfish go into dishes such as *char kway teow* and the Singaporean version of laksa. They are also served cooked with a simple chilli-vinegar dip on the side.

Oysters
(Tiram)
The large, juicy oysters that you may be familiar with are not a common part of Malaysian cuisine, but what you will find are the small variety, which feature in the popular hawker dish *or luah*, also known as *or chien* – fried oyster omelette.

Shrimp
(Udang Geragau)
These tiny shrimp found in the seas off the Straits of Melaka and in the waters of Penang are used to make the condiments *cincalok* and *belacan*. For *cincalok* the shrimp are mixed with rice and salt and left to ferment for three days.

Squid
(Sotong)
Large and medium-sized squid are often stuffed or cut into rings, which can be braised in a chilli sauce or with tamarind or coconut.

Clams
(Kerang)
This shellfish occasionally features as a mildly spicy option at *nasi campur* stalls. Peranakans stir-fry them with curry paste, curry leaves and lemongrass for a dry, spicy dish.

BELACAN
The making of fermented shrimp paste belacan *is a sight to behold and – if you have a strong stomach – a smell to be inhaled. Fresh shrimp is rinsed in seawater and mixed with salt before being left to dry in the sun. Next it is put through a crushing machine, then stored in wooden vats for a week before it is once again laid out to dry and put through the machine. This process is repeated several times. When the paste is ready, it is shaped it into round or rectangular blocks and dried once more before being wrapped in a couple of layers of paper. Lower-grade* belacan *can smell like rotting fish. The good stuff smells like a fresh ocean breeze.*

Left: Ever-popular *kari ayam* (chicken curry)

POULTRY

After fish, *ayam* (chicken) is possibly the most consumed flesh in the region. Free-range *kampong* (village) chicken is prized for its flavour and lean meat, but the reality is that in most dishes the bird is likely to have never left its coop.

Chicken features in many favourite dishes including Hainanese chicken rice; *ayam buah keluak* (a mildly spicy, sour chicken dish made with *buah keluak*, black nuts from Indonesia); *ayam soto* (Malay chicken noodle soup); and *ayam apitan* (a mild Nonya curry dish).

Every bit of the chicken is used. The feet are marinated and served steamed as a dim sum delicacy (in Cantonese this dish poetically translates as 'phoenix claws'), or they are boiled, de-boned and served cold at chicken-rice restaurants as an appetiser. Livers, hearts and gizzards are also offered as side orders at chicken-rice joints, while chicken liver and gizzard curries are common Indian dishes.

Itek (duck) is less frequently consumed. Classic dishes, though, are Peranakan *itek sio* (duck stewed with tamarind and coriander), *itek tim* (duck and salted vegetable soup) and *lor ark* (Teochew braised duck, served with a piquant chilli, Chinese leek and white-vinegar dip). Beijing duck, also known as Peking duck (crisply cooked duck served with small pancakes and julienned cucumber and spring onion) is available at specialist Chinese restaurants in Singapore and major Malaysian cities. At hawker centres you'll often find a roasted meat stall with rows of whole ducks, their skin a glistening dark brown, hanging by their necks in the display cabinet.

SATE

Originally an Indonesian dish, *sate* (pronounced the same as satay) is a massively popular hawker food throughout Malaysia and Singapore. The small wooden skewers of meat, most often chicken or beef, are grilled over charcoal and basted in a sweet oily sauce to keep them moist while cooking.

Also look out for *sate lok-lok* in Penang and *sate celup* in Melaka. In these fusion versions of the dish, rather than being grilled the sticks are cooked in Chinese steamboat style. Pieces of raw meat, tofu, century eggs, quail eggs, fish cake, offal or vegetables are skewered on bamboo sticks, which are cooked by being dipped in boiling water or stock. The *sate* is then eaten with a sweet, dark sauce, sometimes with chilli sauce as an accompaniment. The difference between *sate lok-lok* and *sate celup* is that the latter is cooked in a boiling peanut sauce.

PORK

KONG BAK PAU

While *babi* (pork) is considered haram (forbidden) among Muslims, the Chinese, Peranakans and Eurasians (but not so much the Indians) revel in its flavour. Chinese especially love the fatty layers of belly pork used to make the Hokkien dish *kong bak pau*. The meat is first braised in a rich stock often consisting of dark and light soy sauce, caramelised sugar, Chinese cooking wine, star anise and Chinese cassia bark. Once cooked the pork is sliced into rectangular portions and sandwiched between sliced steamed buns.

BAK KUT TEH

Pork ribs are used to make a peppery, herbal soup called *bak kut teh*, which old men love to sip on while chatting with their friends at neighbourhood coffeeshops. While the soup is the focus of the meal, the tender flesh on the pork ribs is delicious dipped into side dishes containing sliced bird's eye chillies steeped in light soy sauce before being eaten. The spicy sensation of chilli, soy and melt-in-your-mouth pork is absolutely divine.

KWAY CHAP

In typical Chinese fashion, no part of the beast is wasted. *Kway chap* (a Teochew meal of braised pig's offal, pork cuts, hard-boiled eggs, braised tofu and roughly cut sheets of rice noodles) ensures that every bit of pig is used. The more adventurous eaters may also want to sample the glistening, smooth cubes of pig's blood on display. Can't stomach that? Then just ask for slices of pork, braised tofu and hard-boiled eggs in your bowl of rice noodles.

BABI PONG TEH

Peranakans and Eurasians have also got cooking pork down to a fine art. *Babi pong teh* (stewed pork) is a family favourite. Belly pork and bamboo shoots are flavoured with *tau cheo* (fermented soya beans), cinnamon, dark soy sauce and sugar to create this hearty stew that's perfect with a bowl of steamed rice. And their *sek bak* (belly pork in a spicy black sauce),

dipped in just a smidgen of *sambal belacan* (chilli and fermented shrimp paste), is what gastronomic dreams are made of.

FENG

Feng is a special Eurasian dish, often served at Christmas and best eaten after it's been left to sit for a day. Lean pork from the pig's hind legs is used in this curry that requires the addition of a special *feng* curry powder (composed of coriander, cumin and fennel). Because cooking this dish is such a tedious process, a big pot of it is normally prepared early and the required amount reheated when the need arises. It is often served with a baguette-style bread, *achar* (preserved mixed vegetables – a Eurasian *achar* usually consists of cucumber, green chillies, shallots, cabbage, garlic and some ginger in a pickling liquid), fried pork chipolatas (small sausages) and meatball cutlets (minced pork balls).

Left: Hawker cooking *char siu bao* (barbecued-pork buns)

BEEF & MUTTON

Left: Indian mutton curry
Right: Lunch at a Singapore hawker centre

Daging lembu (beef) and *daging kambing* (mutton) are commonly served at a Malay dinner table. Malays use the word *kambing* to refer to both lamb and mutton, as well as to kid and goat.

While Chinese do appreciate stir-fried slivers of beef, the heady aroma of mutton is not as popular. Most Indians in the region are Tamils, and many are strict vegetarians who don't even touch meat. The cow, to Hindus in particular, is considered sacred, and Indians therefore never consume beef. Mutton, on the other hand, is often served in curries and biryanis.

In the Malay kitchen, beef *rendang* (beef in a thick coconut-milk curry sauce), *daging masak kicap* (beef in soy sauce), *gulai daging* (beef curry), *daging asam* (tamarind beef), *serunding daging* (spicy beef floss) and its mutton counterparts fill the home cook's prospective menu.

Older meat (meaning mutton rather than lamb) is usually stewed for a long time to make it most palatable. And don't be surprised when your order of *daging bakar* (grilled beef) comes to you well done, rather than medium-rare, the way you may be used to having your steaks. Beef just isn't served pink here.

UNUSUAL

Above: *Paru goreng* served with rice and sambal

SUP TORPEDO

The key ingredient of this soup is bull's penis. Served at hawker stalls and *mamak* restaurants, the soup is made with chopped up slices of the penis boiled in a broth of shallots, garlic, ginger and other spices. Some chefs will also throw bull's testicles into the mix. You might not be surprised to learn that the soup is believed to act as a natural Viagra for men.

PARU GORENG

Cow lungs is the main protein here, fried along with spices. It's a tasty meat that goes well with rice.

FOODS

While 'unusual' is firmly in the eye of the beholder, there are some foods that the average visitor may find anything but ordinary.

BIRDS-NEST SOUP

Dubbed by some 'the caviar of the East' are swiftlet nests. Created from the dried spit of the birds, these nests are packed with protein and believed by practitioners of traditional Chinese medicine to have several health benefits (none of which have been scientifically proven). These include promoting overall immunity, speeding up recovery, enhancing libido and keeping your skin looking youthful Some 600 tonnes of the nests are harvested each year in Malaysia, both from the caves and gutted old shophouses in which the birds build their nests.

SAGO GRUBS

A delicacy in Sabah and Sarawak are sago grubs, known as *siat* or *butod*. Sago palm is an important crop in Malaysian Borneo. Sago palm weevils lay eggs in the rotting pith of the sago trunk that develop into fat, wriggly grubs the size of a man's little finger. Creamy yellow in colour and rich in protein, the grubs are eaten boiled in soups or stir-fried with shallots and ginger. Those who are brave enough to eat them raw say that the taste is like sweet coconut milk but with a tough, chewy skin.

CENTURY EGG

Also known as thousand-year-old eggs *(pi dan)* this food is made by preserving chicken or duck eggs in a mixture of chalk, ash, salt and rice husks for two to four months. The egg, before the brown sawdust layer and shell are peeled away, has a pungent odour that smells like ammonia. The preservation process turns the egg-white into a thick, translucent black gel, and the yolk is a grey-green colour.

PULSES & SEEDS

Protein-rich soya beans are processed to make various types of tofu, fermented beans and soy sauce – all used in Malaysian and Singaporean dishes. Other commonly vegetable sources of protein include lentils, peas and various types of seeds.

TOFU

Malaysians and Singaporeans know tofu as *taufu* or *tauhu*. The basic bean curd is made from soya beans that have been soaked; puréed or blended, cooked, sieved and then solidified into curds with the addition of a coagulate. The choice of coagulate (which can be salt-, acid- or enzyme-based) used affects the texture of the tofu.

The softest form of tofu is silken tofu. Chopped into small cubes and added to soups, it can also be sliced into discs, then either pan-fried and served with an egg and crab-meat sauce, or individually topped with minced pork and steamed with a light sauce.

A slightly firmer version of tofu is pan-fried and used in dishes such as *tauhu goreng* (fried tofu topped with blanched bean sprouts, slivers of cucumber and a spicy-sweet peanut sauce). *Taukua*, an even firmer tofu, is used to create *taukua pau*, where it is split open to form a pocket and then stuffed with vegetables and pieces of braised duck.

Tau pok is bean curd that has been deep-fried until its insides have been transformed into a spongy hollow. These hollows are often stuffed with fish paste for *yong taufu*, a hawker dish where diners choose items that are then dropped into a soup with noodles. *Tau pok* can also be stuffed with minced meat and added into Eurasian and Peranakan soups.

Tau kee is bean curd in sheets. A skin forms on the surface when bean curd is made, which is removed, dried flat and then folded into sheets which need to be soaked in warm water before use. Peranakan cooks use it in *chap chye* (a mixed vegetable dish), and Chinese use it in stir-fries, braised claypot dishes and soups.

Tau huay (sweet soya-bean curd) is commonly served at hawker stalls, particularly ones that serve *tau huay chwee* (sweet

soya-bean milk). This extremely delicate curd is served in bowls with a sweet syrup drizzled over it.

To make *tau cheo*, cooked soya beans are heavily salted and fermented for over a month. The resulting whole but very soft beans are highly salty. Sold in jars, *tau cheo* adds a salty depth of flavour to dishes and sauces.

BUAH KELUAK

Also known as *pangium edule*, these black, hard-shelled nuts come from the kepayang tree which is native to Malaysia, Singapore and Indonesia. The pitch-black meat of the processed seeds is soft and oily and tastes a bit like a strong mushroom, with the barest hint of truffle.

Preparation of the nuts, which naturally contain hydrogen cyanide, is highly labour-intensive so as to remove their poison. They form the basis of the Peranakan chicken stew dish *ayam buah keluak*.

PULSES

Pulses are the edible seeds of plants in the legume family such as beans, peas and lentils. They form the basis of many an Indian vegetarian dish and are fabulous sources of protein and vitamins. Whether it's black-eyed beans and chickpeas or yellow, red and black lentils, an Indian meal is rarely complete without a *daal* curry, snack or sweet made from pulses.

Dosa, a staple breakfast item, consists of paper-thin rice-and-lentil crêpes served with coconut chutney and curry. Lentils are often used to thicken curries. *Urad dal*, a flour made from ground black lentils, is used to make snacks such as the deep-fried, crispy *murukuu* and flatbreads such as *chapattis*.

TEMPEH

To make this soya-bean cake, boiled soya beans are sprinkled with a yeast starter, shaped into slabs, wrapped in banana leaves and left for around 48 hours to ferment. The fermented beans form a nutritious, low-cholesterol and high-protein food that has a crunchy texture and nutty flavour. It can be pan-fried and served hot with nasi lemak (coconut rice).

Left: Soy sauce is a ubiquitous dip

SOY SAUCE

Alongside chilli sauce, soy sauce (*kicap* in Malay, *jiang you* in Mandarin) is perhaps the most popular type of sauce in Malaysia and Singapore. In markets and at supermarkets there is often a bewildering range of soy sauces to choose from.

Naturally fermented soy sauce is made from boiled soya beans and roasted wheat mixed with a mould culture. It takes several months to produce and the resulting sauce tastes quite different from the mass-produced stuff which is made in only a few days.

Much like the first oil from the olive press that is labelled 'extra virgin' and prized for its flavour, the first extraction of naturally fermented soy sauce is considered the most flavoursome, and has the pure saltiness that you get from tasting the best sea salt.

LIGHT SOY SAUCE

Thinner and saltier than regular or dark soy sauce, this is normally used for dips, marinating ingredients, dressing and stir-frying foods.

DARK SOY SAUCE

Thicker, less salty and aged longer than regular soy sauce, the dark version has a richer flavour and darker colour due to the addition of caramel. It is used in fried noodles and braised pork, chicken, or beef.

KICAP MANIS

This thick soy sauce, sweetened with a generous amount of palm sugar, is a bit like treacle. It is used in *char kway teow* (broad, flat rice-flour noodles stir-fried with Chinese sausage and egg), in *popiah* (Peranakan spring rolls that are not deep-fried) and many Indonesian-influenced dishes.

TAMARI

Tamari is the liquid by-product which forms when making miso (a savoury paste made from fermented soya beans). While soy sauce contains wheat, tamari has little or no wheat – which is why tamari is a great option for anyone who's gluten-free.

CONDIMENTS & SAUCES

Apart from soy, there are many other pre-prepared sauces and condiments that Malaysian and Singaporean cooks keep on hand in the cupboard. The following are the most popular.

HOISIN SAUCE

Made from salted soya beans, sugar, vinegar, sesame oil and spices such as five-spice and star anise, hoisin is used as a dipping sauce. It's also deployed as a meat glaze and in marinades, and spread over Peking duck pancakes before they are rolled.

OYSTER SAUCE

This thick, dark brown, umami flavouring, a Cantonese speciality, is made from oysters which have been boiled down to an extract. This is then cooked further with cornflour, sugar, salt and caramel to create the sauce. It is generally used at the end of a stir-fry (to top stir-fried vegetables, for example), as part of a marinade or as a dipping sauce.

From far left: Peking duck is served with hoisin sauce; Oyster sauce adds flavour to stir-fried vegetables

FISH SAUCE

Fish sauce is made from anchovies and is extremely salty and strong smelling. In Thailand it is known as *nam pla* and is often used in Thai dishes or as a dip with chopped bird's eye chillies. In Malaysia and Singapore it is more often used to season foods such as fried rice and noodles.

KETCHUP

You'd be amazed at the amount of ketchup (tomato sauce or *sos tomato* in Malay) that's used by everyone. It appears in dishes as disparate as Hainanese pork chops (as part of the sweet-and-sour sauce), Singapore chilli crab, Indian *mee goreng* (a spicy fried noodle dish), *wonton mee* (*wonton* noodle soup) and *nasi tomato* (tomato-flavoured rice served with a variety of dishes).

CHILLI SAUCE

Commercial chilli sauces tend to be a little sweet, and some have added garlic. These sauces are sometimes used to flavour meals quickly, but more often appear as dips for anything from fried chicken wings and deep-fried spring rolls to French fries. Thai sweet chilli sauce is more sweet than spicy, and has visible pieces of chopped chilli floating in a semi-translucent sauce.

ORIGINS OF KETCHUP

An interesting theory is that the word ketchup comes from ke-tsiap – an old Chinese fish sauce brought to ports like Melaka and Penang by Chinese traders and settlers centuries ago. Kicap *(pronounced 'kichap') is also Malay for soy sauce.*

FLAVOURINGS

Malaysian and Singaporean cooks are masters of flavour. From the warm earthiness of garlic, turmeric and ginger to the citrusy kick of lemongrass and coriander and the gentle sweetness of pandan leaves, they know how to perfectly balance ingredients to create supreme taste sensations.

ONIONS

There are a few types of *bawang* (onions) that are commonly used in the region. *Bawang merah* is a tiny red shallot that grows in clumps similar to garlic. It is either pounded or ground to form part of a *rempah* in numerous local dishes. It's far more pungent than white or brown onions and adds a distinctive aroma and flavour to dishes.

The slightly larger red *bawang besar* (Bombay onion) is chopped and served raw with satay, and used in most dishes, although brown onion is commonly used in its place. *Daun bawang* (spring onions/scallions) are widely used in Chinese cooking, with the green tops often finely chopped, or cut into slivers, and used as a garnish. *Koo chai* (chives) are sprinkled as a garnish over some noodle dishes.

TAMARIND

Asam jawa is the pulp obtained from the tamarind pod of the *Tamarindus indica* tree, and packets of this are commonly available. Tamarind juice is obtained by soaking the pulp in warm water. This is used in curries and soups to create a sour taste and is central to the sourness of *mee siam* (a spicy, tangy noodle dish). *Asam gelugur* (dried tamarind slices), while offering a similar sourness, do not provide the full flavour of *asam jawa*. They are made from a different product altogether and are sun-dried slices of the fruit of the *asam gelugur* tree (*Garcinia atroviridis).*

GINGER

Halia (fresh ginger) provides a subtle heat to dishes and is believed to have medicinal qualities. It is minced and served with a fresh chilli paste with Hainanese chicken rice; steamed with fish; crushed in *rempahs*; and even used in *teh halia* (milky ginger tea).

GARLIC

Bawang putih (garlic) is as essential to the spice paste *rempah* as shallots. It is used with near wild abandon in curries, soups (in vast quantities in *bak kut teh* – pork rib soup), and meat and vegetable dishes. No one ever worries about having garlic breath.

GALANGAL

Lengkuas (galangal, also known as blue ginger) looks like ginger but has pungent citrusy flavour and aroma. Galangal should be used sparingly as it imparts a bitter taste if too much is used.

KAFFIR LIME LEAVES

Daun limau purut, the fresh leaves of the kaffir lime tree are used, finely shredded, in Peranakan and Eurasian – as well as some Malay – curries and *sambals*. The leaves have a delicate lime smell and impart a subtle flavour.

Above: A variety of foods and flavours feature in even the simplest family meal

From left: *Ais kacang*'s many ingredients include *gula melaka;* Pretty butterfly pea flower iced tea

GULA MELAKA

Gula melaka (palm sugar) is extracted from the stalks of the sugar palm, then boiled and allowed to solidify in the hollow of bamboo poles (which accounts for its cylindrical shape). The rich, musky, near bittersweet flavour of palm sugar can nearly be matched by dark brown or muscovado sugar, but nothing tastes quite like the real thing. The sugar is often melted down into a syrup and used to sweeten desserts such as *cendol* (coconut milk with green noodles), *ais kacang* (a shaved-ice dessert) and *sago gula melaka* (sago pearls with coconut milk sauce). It is also used to sweeten cakes and *kuih* (Malay and Peranakan cakes).

LEMONGRASS

Serai (lemongrass) lends its delightful citrus aroma to curries, soups and tea. It is the lower, bulbous stem that is used (the leaves may only be used for infusions). The tougher outer layers of the stem are discarded, leaving only the pale inner portion that is sliced thinly or simply bruised. Used primarily for flavour and generally not eaten.

CURRY LEAVES

Daun kari (curry leaves) are usually the first ingredient to be tossed into heated oil before the rest of the ingredients in a curry are added. Its small and pointed leaves have a unique flavour and smell, and were introduced to Malaysia by Indian migrants.

TURMERIC

Kunyit (turmeric) is a ginger-like fresh rhizome that is bright orange in colour and has a slightly bitter flavour (be careful not to use too much of it). A slice of fresh turmeric added to rice or curry will give it a bright yellow hue and it is often used in place of saffron. Turmeric is also commonly used in powdered form.

PANDAN LEAVES

Daun pandan (pandan leaf, also known as screwpine leaf) is used to flavour and colour cakes, drinks, rice and desserts. Fresh whole leaves kept in cupboards are believed to keep cockroaches away and in local taxis you may notice that large bunches of pandan leaves are used to impart a pleasant aroma.

CORIANDER/ CILANTRO

The roots of the fresh herb *daun ketumbar* (coriander/cilantro) are pounded and often incorporated into *rempahs* and used to flavour stocks. The fresh leaves are used as a wonderfully fragrant garnish over most curries, fried noodle dishes, steamed fish and even chicken rice.

LAKSA LEAVES

Daun kesum (laksa leaf, also known as Vietnamese coriander) resembles mint although it isn't of the mint family. It has narrow pointed leaves and is strikingly dark green. It is most commonly chopped and tossed over laksa (a spicy, soupy noodle dish) as a garnish.

BUTTERFLY OR BLUE PEA FLOWER

Bunga telang is a tiny, deep-blue (almost violet) flower used to create the natural blue colouring for many Malay, Peranakan and Eurasian desserts and rice dishes. It gives the Kelantan speciality, nasi kerabu (cooked rice tossed with finely shredded herbs) its bluish hue. A handful of flowers are boiled in water and then squeezed. The water is strained and the resulting liquid is used for cooking.

COCONUT

Coconuts (*kelapa* in Malay) are Malaysia's fourth-largest industrial crop behind oil palm, rubber and rice, with most of the plantations found in Sabah and Sarawak. The crop is harvested to make coconut oil, milk, drinks and, of course, for the nuts' white flesh.

COCONUT WATER
(Air Kelapa)

Coconuts take a year to fully ripen. At eight months the liquid, or coconut water, inside the shell is sweet and refreshing and the white flesh is still soft and sticky. You'll often find these young, fresh coconuts being sold at hawker stalls and markets. The tops are lopped off with a cleaver to access the water inside; after finishing your drink, use the removed section of husk to scoop out the soft flesh.

COCONUT MILK
(Santan)

Coconut milk, which is extracted from the grated flesh of coconuts is used to add richness to Malay and Peranakan curries and dishes such as *nasi lemak* (coconut rice) *rendang* and desserts and drinks. In traditional food markets, you'll often hear the loud mechanical whirr of coconut-grating machines that sound like whole coconuts going round in a tumble dryer. The white floss that comes out of the machine is mixed with warm water to release its milky richness; the mixture is then sieved to extract the liquid and the moist pulp squeezed to create a richer milk.

GRATED COCONUT
(Kelapa Parut)

Grated coconut is often used in desserts and cakes, such as to coat the outside of *onde onde* (pandan-flavoured rice balls filled with *gula melaka*) or cooked with *gula melaka* to make a sweet filling for *kuih dadar*.

KERISIK

Grated coconut flesh is toasted and ground to a paste in a mortar and pestle to make a rich, caramelly coconut butter known as *kerisik*. It's used to thicken curries and add flavour to dishes such as *rendang*. The best *kerisik* is freshly made at home; if bought ready-made from shops, look for 'A' grade as this is the most fragrant and creamy form, with a sweet taste and nutty aftertaste. In a more granular form, *kerisik* is used as a condiment in rice dishes such as *nasi ulam* and *nasi kerabu*.

OiLS & SPiCES

Corn oil is most commonly used for pan-frying, stir-frying and deep-frying in local kitchens. But as locals grow more health conscious they are also turning to soya-bean oil and canola oil. The most important thing is that the oil does not impart its own flavour to the dish (the way olive oil would). However, for extra flavour, Chinese cooks might add a little lard (pork fat), while Indian cooks prefer *ghee* (clarified butter) or butter.

SESAME OIL

Minyak bijan in Malay, *ma you* in Cantonese, this nutty oil is pressed from toasted sesame seeds. When heated, it burns easily so is never used for frying. Instead, it is most commonly tossed into dishes (such as noodles) or incorporated into dressings that are poured over poached chicken or steamed fish.

SPICES

As the region was positioned along the Spice Route in the early 1400s, its people naturally experimented with the exotic aromatics that visiting merchants brought with them. *Ketumbar* (coriander powder), *jintan putih* (cumin seeds), *jintan manis* (fennel seeds), *bunga cengkih* (cloves), *kayu manis* (cinnamon), *buah pelaga* (cardamom), *lada* (peppercorns), *serbuk kunyit* (turmeric powder), *serbuk halia* (ginger powder) and *bunga lawing* (star anise) are some of the familiar spices used in local cooking.

FIVE-SPICE POWDER

Serbuk lima rempah (five-spice powder) is a Chinese mixed spice usually containing star anise, cassia bark (with a taste similar to cinnamon), cloves, Sichuan pepper and fennel seeds. It sometimes also includes cardamom, coriander seeds, dried orange peel and ginger powder (yes, that would make it more than five spices, despite its name). Not to be mistaken for allspice, five-spice (or five-fragrance) powder is used in Chinese braised dishes (including braised goose and braised belly pork), *ngoh hiang* (pork or prawn rolls) and *siu yoke* (crispy belly pork).

GARAM MASALA

Essential to many Indian dishes, garam masala is a mixture of ground spices that are either incorporated into the dish or sprinkled over it just before serving. It is generally a mixture of four to six spices, but up to 15 can be included in the mix – coriander seeds and cumin seeds are always included. In northern India, black pepper, cinnamon, cloves and cardamom are added to the mix, while in southern India some of the spices are replaced by chilli and turmeric.

Left: Asian eggplant and winter melon
Right: Bunches of bright green stink beans

VEGETABLES

Plenty of locally grown vegetables, including *bendi* (okra, or ladies' fingers), *terung* (Asian aubergine/eggplant) and bok choy (Chinese white cabbage) are no longer exotic to an international audience. But there are other *sayur* (vegetables) that you might not be familiar with.

CUCUMBER
(Timun)

Unlike the English cucumber, which is dark green, long and fairly skinny, local *timun* are short, thick and have a light green variegated skin. The seeds are also larger and the flesh feels spongier, as if they contain more water. *Timun* are often eaten raw in salads or served shredded as a topping. They are also pickled in Malay, Peranakan and Eurasian *achars* (preserved mixed vegetables).

BITTER GOURD
(Peria)

This long, ridged green gourd comes from a climbing plant. Malays slice it thinly and fry it with shrimp, while Chinese fry it in an omelette (believing it is cooling for the body) or stuff it with fish paste for *yong taufu*.

WATER SPINACH
(Kangkong)

With a hollow stem and large, arrowhead (or heart-shaped, depending on how you look at it) leaves, *kangkong* (also known as water convolvulus) is a popular vegetable often served fried with *sambal belacan* (chilli and *belacan* paste).

YAM BEAN
(Sengkuang)

Also known as jicama and Mexican turnip, the white, mildly sweet, juicy flesh of this tuber is often eaten raw in salads. When cooked, it is one of the major ingredients in the cooked vegetable stuffing that is served with *popiah* (Peranakan spring rolls that are not deep-fried).

SALTED MUSTARD GREENS
(Kiam Chye)

Introduced by the Chinese, *kiam chye* is now also used sparingly in Peranakan and Eurasian soups. It's sliced and added to Malay fish curries to give them that slightly sour zing, but its flavour comes to full force in *itek tim* (duck and salted vegetable soup).

WINTER MELON
(Dong Gua)

Also known as wax gourd, this is technically a fruit. It comes in round or elongated shapes (similar to the different shapes of watermelons) and has translucent flesh rather like that of cucumber. It's prepared in the same way as a regular melon, with its central seeds and membrane scraped out to leave the remaining flesh ready to eat. The cooked flesh offers more texture than flavour to dishes. Candied and dried, it has a distinct flavour akin to caramelised sugar.

STINK BEANS
(Petai)

The long, twisted pods of the petai tree split open to reveal seeds that look like big green broad beans. The beans have a pungent but not especially stinky aroma which lingers in the body a bit like asparagus. Young tender pods can be eaten whole and raw. The beans are usually stir-fried, roasted or stewed with fish.

OTHER GREEN VEGETABLES

Other commonly eaten vegetables include *choy sum* (Chinese flowering cabbage), *gai lan* (Chinese broccoli or kale) and *por choy* (Chinese spinach). These are added to stir-fries, or simply tossed into soups and fried noodle dishes.

FRUiTS

Fruit such as *nenas* (pineapple), watermelon, papaya and green guava are available year-round. April and May are mango months, while from April to September, follow your nose to sample notoriously odoriferous love-it-or-hate-it durian.

DURiAN

Due to its intense odour and spiky appearance, the durian is possibly Southeast Asia's most infamous fruit, the flesh of which can suggest everything from custard to onions. Love it or hate it, it's near impossible to stay neutral about the 'king of fruit'. The creamy, bittersweet flesh is eaten fresh, as *durian pengat* (a porridge-like sweet with coconut cream and palm sugar), piped into choux puffs, slathered onto cakes, or turned into polite – ie, not so stinky – tubes of *durian kuih*, a chewy snack with a fudge-like consistency.

The selection process for the fruit can be mind-boggling as there are so many different varieties, with jargon-like names. The most well-known type is the bright yellow Musang King, which is famed for its rich, creamy flesh that is both bitter and sweet in the mouth. D24 is a pale yellow fruit with a slight kick of alcohol-like flavour. The Red Prawn variety is noticeably sweeter.

JACKFRUiT
(Nangka)

Considered the world's largest fruit, jackfruit takes the form of a giant green pod with dozens of waxy yellow sections. The bumpy shell emits an unappealing odour, and when it's cut open, it oozes a sticky sap. But the jackfruit's bright yellow flesh is sugary sweet and wonderfully fragrant, reminding some of Juicy Fruit chewing gum. The flesh is sometimes boiled, sliced thinly and tossed in a spicy salad (flavoured with *sambal belacan*) called *kerabu nangka*, or added into curries such as *ikan tenggiri masak nangka* (braised mackerel fillet with coconut milk and jackfruit). The *biji nangka* (jackfruit seeds) are often cooked in curry dishes, and they taste a little like potatoes.

SAPODiLLA
(Ciku)

The dull-brown skin of the sapodilla hides supersweet flesh that tastes a bit like a date.

Right: A rainbow of tropical fruit on display

STARFRUIT
(Belimbing)
So named because the cross section of this sweet and tangy fruit resembles a star. It is eaten ripe (locals also like it blended into a juice) or half-ripe, flavoured with a little salt.

LONGAN
(Mata Kucing)
A small fruit with a thin rind that you peel way to find segmented, perfumed pearlescent flesh with a lychee-like flavour. The *langskat* species of this fruit come from northern Peninsular Malaysia while the easier-to-peel *duku* species is from southern peninsula Malaysia.

CUSTARD APPLE
(Buah Nona)
This fruit's knobbly green skin conceals hard, black seeds and sweet, gloopy flesh with a granular texture. Locals enjoy it sliced and dipped in a combination of dark soy sauce and sliced chillies.

SNAKESKIN FRUIT
(Buah Salak)
It's known as the snakeskin fruit because of its scaly skin; the exterior looks like a mutant strawberry and the soft flesh tastes like unripe bananas.

LIMES
While lemons are not common in Malaysian cooking, limes are. The two main types are limau nipis (key limes), often used for making drinks; and the smaller, more orange-fleshed limau kasturi (calamansi limes) which are squeezed over food and into recipes to provide a sour citrus tang.

DRAGON FRUIT
(Buah Naga)
Dragon fruit is easily identifiable by its bright fuchsia skin and wispy green tendrils. Peel the skin and bite into the lightly sweet white or pink flesh

SOURSOP
(Durian Belanda)
Translating from the Malay as 'Dutch durian', this fruit has a fragrant but tart granular flesh and hard, black seeds; it's only ripe when soft and goes off within days, so eat it quickly.

POMELO
(Limau Bali)
Like a grapefruit on steroids, pomelo has a thick pithy green skin hiding sweet, tangy segments; cut into the skin, peel off the pith then break open the segments and munch on the flesh inside.

MANGOSTEEN
(Manggis)
About the size of a tennis ball, a hard, purple shell conceals the mangosteen's delightfully fragrant white segments, some containing a tough seed that you spit out.

BREADFRUIT
(Cempedak)
The Malaysian breadfruit is a huge green fruit with skin like the Thing from the *Fantastic Four*; the seeds and flesh are often curried or fried.

ROSE APPLE
(Jambu Merah)
An elongated pink or red fruit with a smooth, shiny skin and pale, watery flesh. It's a good thirst quencher on a hot day.

RAMBUTAN
A relative of the lychee, this fruit has a red, hairy and leathery shell containing sweet, translucent flesh, which you scrape off from the seed with your teeth.

KUIH

These traditional Malay and Peranakan cakes come in both sweet and savoury versions. Made with rice flour and coconut milk, they can be steamed, baked, fried or boiled and are mostly gluten-free or vegan.

Kuih can refer to cakes, cookies, dumplings, puddings, biscuits and pastries. The word derives from a Chinese character which means 'rice cake' and which is pronounced in Hokkien as 'kway'. You might also see the word spelled *kueh*. Recipes have been passed down through the generations, picking up influences here and there from all the cultures of the Malay Archipelago.

Kuih Denderam

Also known as *peneram*, these are deep-fried rings of dough made from rice flour, palm sugar and coconut milk. The inspiration is said to have been the Indian snack *adhirasam,* where the dough is fla-voured with ginger and cardamom.

Kuih Bakar

It's the pandan leaf, the region's equivalent of vanilla, that provides the distinctive green hue and fragrant aroma and taste of this baked egg and coconut custard cake. A nice touch is the caramelised sesame seed-encrusted topping.

Rempeyek

Originally from Indonesia, these savoury deep-fried crackers are made from a batter of rice flour, coconut milk and water. They are usually studded with peanuts, dried anchovies *(ikan bilis)* and cumin seeds.

Dodol

This toffee-like sweet is made with coconut milk, glutinous rice flour and *gula melaka*. It can take anything up to 12 hours to cook down the mixture in a wok to the required firm, slightly sticky consistency.

Ang Ku Kuih

Meaning 'red tortoise cake' in Hokkien, *ang ku kuih* have a bright orange-red skin made from glutinous rice flour and a mung bean paste filling. They can also come in other shades with fillings such as crushed peanuts and shredded coconut.

Onde Onde

Originating in Indonesia, this *kuih* has become a favourite of Nonya cooks. Balls of glutinous rice dough, coloured green with pandan, are wrapped around a spoonful of semi-melted *gula melaka*. They are finally coated with freshly shredded coconut.

Kuih Lapis

Lapis means 'layer' in Malay, and that accurately describes this pudding-like cake which is made from steamed, differently coloured layers of rice-flour batter. All sorts of colour combinations are possible, but you'll often see white, red and green.

Putu Piring

Also known as *kuih tutu*, these fluffy, steamed rice-flour cakes are filled with *gula melaka*. They are usually cooked in stainless steel moulds shaped like a cone or flower.

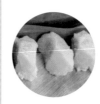

Kuih Jagung

The thick yellow layer on top of this cake is a set custard made with canned sweetcorn. The thinner bottom layer of white is coconut milk with pandan.

Kuih Ketayap

Also known as *kuih dadar*, these spongy pandan crêpes, rolled up with a filling of shredded coconut, are best eaten warm off the pan.

DRiNKS

Right: A vendor skilfully 'pulling' *teh tarik*

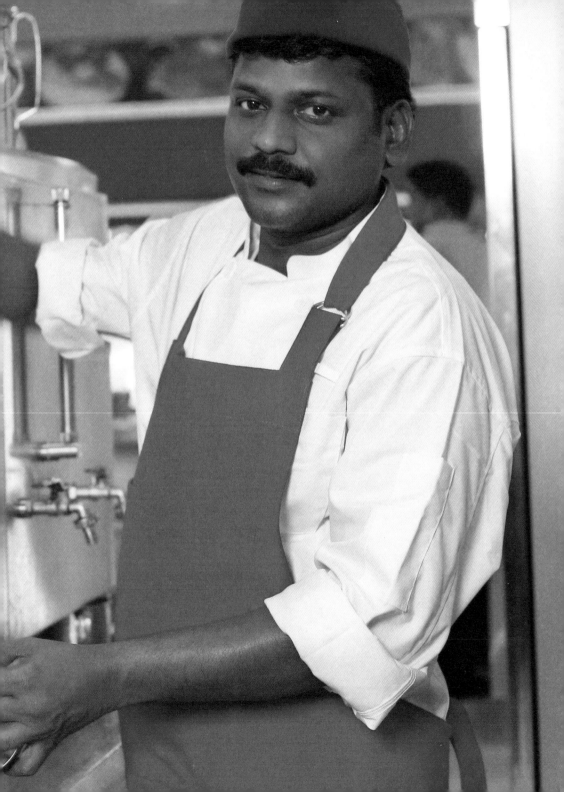

TEA

Malaysians and Singaporeans are inveterate tea drinkers. Any time is tea time in the region and the drink is available around every corner, from the cheapest *mamak* (Indian Muslim) stall serving *teh tarik* (pulled tea) to the hushed ambiance of a traditional Chinese tea house.

TEA PLANTATIONS

The people of the Malay Peninsula have a long history of enjoying tea. In Kedah State's Bujang Valley, the richest archaeological area in Malaysia, tea-related artefacts dating back to the 8th century BCE have been found. Chinese immigrants also brought their tea-drinking culture with them when they began to arrive in Melaka from the 15th century onwards. However, tea drinking really began to take off among the local population during British colonisation.

In 1929 John Archibald Russell teamed up with AB Milne, a veteran planter from Sri Lanka, to start a tea plantation 1500m (4920ft) above sea level in Perak State's Cameron Highlands. With an average temperature of 18°C (64°F), plenty of sunshine and mildly acidic soil, the Cameron Highlands are perfect for growing the tea bush *Camellia sinensis*. Today, Malaysia produces about 3.6 million kg (7.9 million lb) of black tea annually from its three major tea estates, those owned by Boh and Bharat in the Cameron Highlands and Sabah Tea on the lower slopes of Mt Kinabalu in Sabah.

TEA VARIETIES

The dominant variety grown and used is the Indian Assam tea, *Camellia assamica*. The total annual demand far exceeds local production, so the balance is imported (some imports are considered inferior, others superior). Locals take great pride in knowing exactly where they can find the best tea (and coffee) made the local way.

Be prepared for a unique taste sensation when you sip on your first local *teh*, which you can only find at coffeeshops and hawker drink stalls. This style of tea is rarely prepared at home. Unlike the delicate teas of China and Japan, which are served plain, or even British-style tea served with milk, Malaysian and Singaporean tea is brewed for longer to give it stronger flavour. It is typically served with thick condensed milk, which is both sweet and rich. This style of tea preparation has its roots in the tea-making methods practised in India, where tea is infused with a mixture of water and milk.

Left: Frothy *teh tarik*
Right: Chinese tea poured in elegant, thimble-sized cups

TEH TARIK (PULLED TEA)

A style of tea that is unique to the region is *teh tarik* (literally 'pulled tea'). The act of making the tea has become part of the tourism landscape, but it is nonetheless a visual experience not to be missed. The art of 'pulling' tea is widely regarded as an amazing display of showmanship, so much so that Malaysia often holds competitions for stylistic skills, with competitors putting on acrobatic shows to a musical accompaniment.

Teh tarik originated from British colonial times when Indian-Muslim immigrants set up drinks stands for the workers at rubber plantations. This is why the *teh tarik* master is invariably Indian, and you should really only order at an Indian drink stall. His unique art involves pouring your tea – sweetened with condensed milk – from a metal container held high above his head down into another metal container he holds somewhere close to his waist level (the two should be about 1m/3ft apart). The process is repeated a couple of times until a layer of froth appears and the

tea has cooled a little. He then pours your drink into a cup. The benefit of this process is that the drink is cooled just enough not to burn your tongue when you sip it.

Be aware that iced tea served at *kopitiam* (coffeeshops) will invariably be a local tea (yes, with the condensed milk) served with ice. Modern East-meets-West concoctions include *teh-cino* (inspired by cappuccino), which is a tea served with a bottom-half layer of milky tea and a top half that is frothy and milky white. For full effect, it's served in a glass mug, of course. If you're feeling a little under the weather, ask for a cup of *teh halia* (milky ginger tea). It's a restorative pick-me-up that most locals swear by.

CHINESE TEAS

Each of the different dialect groups of Chinese brought with them to Malaysia and Singapore tastes for different types of teas: green tea for the Hakka, oolong tea for the Hokkien, and the aged black teas *lui pao* and *pu erh* for the Cantonese. All of these, as well as

jasmine tea and others, are available in Chinese tea shops in Kuala Lumpur, Singapore, George Town on the island of Penang and Melaka City as well as in upmarket Chinese restaurants.

The more stylish the restaurant, the more likely you are to find exquisite, rare teas. Generally, Chinese tea, served in small teacups containing little more than a thimble-full of liquid, is designed to be appetite-enhancing (if served at the beginning of a meal) or cleansing (if served at the end of a meal). Pale-yellow chrysanthemum tea is often served sweet.

OTHER TEAS

Japanese restaurants will have *sencha* (green tea) and maybe some other types of Japanese tea such as *hojicha* (roasted green tea) and *matcha* (powdered green tea). At Indian restaurants, you can indulge in a rich *masala* (spice blend) tea that is milky, sweet and spiced with cardamom, cloves and cinnamon. Tea served the British way, either plain or with a drop of milk, is readily available. Specialised teahouses focusing on herbal teas (such as camomile, lavender and mint) are growing in popularity as are places serving bubble tea, a hit import from Taiwan where a tea mixed with perhaps milk and fruit juices is served with tapioca pearls (the bubbles).

MILK IN YOUR DRINK

Depending on how you like your coffee or tea, it's worth understanding the different types of milks used to make these drinks in Malaysia and Singapore. A regular kopi *or* teh *is made with condensed milk while* kopi-c *or* teh-c *is made with evaporated milk. The difference between condensed and evaporated milk is the amount of sugar in the liquid – condensed milk is sweeter.*

151

KOPI (COFFEE)

The third-wave coffee revolution has washed over Malaysia and Singapore, making single-origin beans and siphon brews all the rage among local hipsters. However, old-school *kopitiam* (coffeeshops) continue to deliver the real local deal, and this still holds sway.

Despite being in the 'bean belt' (the horizontal strip around the world where coffee can be cultivated), Malaysia isn't renowned as an origin for the bean. Coffee production volumes are low, and they have been steadily declining since the late 20th century for a variety of reasons – including increased labour costs and the emergence of more lucrative agricultural products such as palm oil.

Malaysia also specialises in growing liberica – the third most popular species in the *Coffea* genus after arabica and robusta – comprising less than 1% of all coffee grown worldwide. Most of this coffee is consumed locally in a blend with robusta beans that is roasted with palm-oil margarine and sugar to impart a rich, buttery aroma and flavour. The resulting coffee drink is characterised by a heavy body, earthiness and a mellow smoothness.

At a traditional *kopitiam* you will not find espressos, lattes or flat whites on the menu. Instead, the locally roasted and ground beans form the basis of a whole different range of coffee drinks (see opposite). You'll find locals start and end their days with a coffee. The old-timers prefer to pour some of their piping hot coffee into saucers to hasten the cooling process before casually sipping the dark, smoky brew from the lips of the little dishes. On a hot day, a *kopi-peng* (iced coffee served with condensed milk) offers the perfect relief from the heat and the sun.

MY LIBERICA

Founded in 2011, My Liberica claims to be Malaysia's 'first speciality liberica producer'. This Johor-based plantation (located in the region of Malaysia where most coffee is cultivated) has its own small chain of coffeeshops, serving their natural, washed and honey-processed liberica beans. The naturals are winey, with flavours of jackfruit, while the honeys can taste of hazelnut and chocolate.

Kopitiam Drink Decoder

KOPI
Coffee (80%)
+ condensed milk (20%)

TEH
Tea (80%)
+ condensed milk (20%)

KOPI-O/TEH-O
Black coffee/tea (90%)
+ sugar (10%)

KOPI-C/TEH-C
Coffee/tea (75%)
+ evaporated milk (15%)
+ sugar (10%)

KOPI-MIN-TIM/ TEH-MIN-TIM
Less sweet coffee/tea (90%)
+ condensed milk (10%)

KOPI-O KOSONG/ TEH-O KOSONG
Coffee/tea (100%)

CHAM
Coffee (45%)
+ Tea (45%)
+ condensed milk (10%)

KOPI-PENG/ TEH-PENG
Coffee/tea (80%) +
condensed milk (20%) + ice

TEH TARIK
Frothy 'pulled' tea; can
also be made with coffee

TEH HALIA
Tea with ginger juice

FRUIT JUICES

Beat the heat and keep up your daily vitamin intake by sipping the freshly made juices that are readily available at hawker centres and food courts. Look out for colourful displays of cut fruit and the whirr of a juicer going at full speed.

Familiar options include watermelon, orange, apple (red or green) and pineapple. A local favourite is a mix of carrot and orange juice. More local options include sugar cane juice, which is extracted from the cane with a purpose-built press and is an amazing thirst-quencher when served with a wedge of lemon; star fruit; and soursop, a dark green, prickly fruit with a slightly acidic, tropical-flavoured pulp (the seeds are not meant to be consumed).

More recent – and somewhat exotic – additions to the selection cover anything from honeydew with milk, which first made it big in Taiwan, to the rich, Indonesian-influenced avocado with a hint of instant coffee. Be warned that most stalls add a generous tablespoon of sugar syrup and some tend to fill your glass up with ice (which leaves you with more ice than juice). Feel free to request that they don't add sugar to your juice. A request for 'no ice' will usually incur a surcharge.

LIME JUICE

Lime juice is another common option at fruit juice stalls, and you are likely to find it on the menus of coffeeshops. Don't cringe at the thought of drinking it. In taste, it's closer to a refreshing lemonade rather than a pure, astringent juice. That's because the limes used to make it are often calamansi (also known as *limau kasturi* in Malay), which are a hybrid of a citrus fruit and a kumquat. They are two-thirds the size of a golf ball with pale orange flesh.

The sweetness of the drink, which is nearly always enhanced with sugar syrup, is believed to soothe the palate after a spicy meal, and its ever-so-slightly sour bite also cleanses the palate after a rich, greasy meal the way a lemon or lime sorbet would. At larger establishments, the 'fresh' juice is often either a cordial or a commercially extracted product; hand-squeezing those little limes is far too time-consuming to be commercially viable.

You may also come across a variation referred to as *limau asam boi* in Malay, *kat chai suen mui* in Cantonese and *guai bee* in Hokkien. This drink is lime juice mixed with a few dried, sour salted plums (*asam boi* in Malay) that have been soaked in a sugar solution. Sweet, sour and just a little salty, it's a super-refreshing concoction that hits the spot after a long day spent pounding the streets and taking in the sights.

From far left: Jelly-filled *air cincau*; Street stalls sell vibrantly coloured drinks

COCONUT JUICE (Air Kelapa)

While coconut juice isn't exactly a juice – the liquid you drink isn't extracted in any way, the nut is simply cracked open and the liquid in it offered to you – it is a drink that would most logically fall under the category of juices. Also known as coconut water, it is mildly sweet and provides a soothingly pleasant counterpoint to spicy food. It is usually available at roadside stalls (where you'll see green, whole coconuts on display) and most hawker centres (especially the ones that cater to tourists). The tops are trimmed to a three-cornered point and with the swish of a cleaver, the tip is removed to reveal a pool of liquid and a layer of tender white flesh. You drink the liquid and then, with the aid of a metal spoon, scrape off the flesh, which can be eaten – as long as it's a fairly young coconut that you've been given. It'll have the delicate flavour of coconut, but without the richness that you've come to associate with coconut milk or cream. Other places serve the juice in a glass, with the coconut flesh scraped out and mixed through the juice (which is handy if you intend to walk with drink in hand).

STREET— STALL DRINKS

The only advertising that drink stalls need is a display of distinctively coloured local drinks laid out in tall, transparent containers. You're likely to be able to tell which drinks they sell from a long way down the road.

AIR BANDUNG

Possibly the most eye-catching drink available, this milky-pink thirst quencher is made from a combination of rose syrup (a commercial product consisting of rose essence, sugar syrup and pink colouring) and evaporated or condensed milk. It makes a great accompaniment to Malay food. You should only drink this cold.

CHIN CHOW/ GRASS JELLY DRINK

(Air Cincau)

This ebony-coloured drink filled with strands of black jelly is considered a great herbal tonic. The jelly is made from *agar-agar* (a gelatine-like substance obtained from seaweed) and *chin chow* (a type of Chinese cabbage) leaf, which can be bought at Chinese medicinal shops. The liquid consists of sugar syrup flavoured with pandan leaf. Ready-made *chin chow* jelly, as well as canned versions of the drink, can be bought at supermarkets. Some prefer to have it with a hint of fresh lemon juice.

SOYA-BEAN MILK

(Air Soya)

Soya-bean milk consists of beans that have been liquidised with water and then strained, before being boiled and sweetened with sugar. Very different to the soy milk you're likely to find in health food stores both locally and overseas, it has a beany flavour that is usually masked with the addition of pandan leaves at the boiling stage. A popular drink served both hot and cold, you are likely to find many stalls selling this milky white liquid. Because it's rich in protein, many locals choose to drink a glass of it each day. Soy milk in cans and cartons can also be found in most supermarkets.

BARLEY WATER (Air Barli)

This refreshing drink is made from barley boiled with water to create a murky, white liquid, and its primary flavouring comes from the rock sugar dissolved in it as it boils. When consumed at home, *dong gua* (candied winter melon) is sometimes added, creating a caramelised-sugar bittersweetness (akin to the flavour of molasses). It can be served either hot or cold. As a canned drink, lemon-barley is a popular combination.

LONGAN WATER OR TEA (Air Mata Kucing)

The Chinese serve *air mata kucing* during the Chinese New Year. Despite sometimes being called a tea, this ultra-sweet beverage doesn't actually contain any tea leaves. It is a combination of *kurma* (red dates) and dried *mata kucing* (longan) boiled in water. It is the sweet, dried longan (similar to lychee) that gives the drink its amber-brown hue. You'll also find a chilled version of the drink sold at roadside stalls and markets (there's a famous stall in Kuala Lumpur's Petaling Street Market). Some hawkers claim that they add secret herbs that make their version of *air mata kucing* even more of a tonic

CENDOL

Midway between a dessert and a drink is cendol. *The liquid element is coconut milk (where the flesh of the coconut is grated and squeezed to produce a milk) sweetened with palm-sugar syrup – the freshness of the coconut milk and the quality of the palm sugar can make or break a* cendol. *Approximately a quarter of your glass or bowl is first filled with fine, short strings of cooked green-bean-flour dough (the finer the strings, the better quality the* cendol). *The palm-sugar syrup is then added, followed by the coconut milk, and then topped with some shaved ice. So be sure to give your* cendol *a good stir before you sip it! Either suck the little noodles up your straw (if you're drinking it out of a mug), or spoon them, along with the sweet liquid, and chew.*

Left: Rose-flavoured *air bandung*

Right: Supermarkets stock a huge choice of soft drinks

OTHER SOFT DRINKS

Alongside freshly prepared thirst quenchers, there is no shortage of canned or bottled soft drinks. You'll find a wide range in supermarkets, convenience stores and street stalls, including all the popular international brands. Favourites among locals include Fanta Orange, Kickapoo (grapefruit based) and Sarsi (sarsaparilla flavoured). You'll also discover a host of fizzy apple juices from China, fruit-based soft drinks from Japan and other local drink products. Non-fizzy options include canned versions of popular drinks sold at roadside stalls. Other interesting variations include jasmine tea (served sweet and cold), winter melon tea (which is essentially candied winter melon boiled in water) and chrysanthemum tea (made by steeping dried chrysanthemums in boiling water, sweetening it and serving it cold in the can).

NUTMEG JUICE

A drink you might only find on the west coast Malaysian island of Penang is *jus pala* (nutmeg juice). Nutmeg trees were introduced to Penang during British colonial times. Here it is the flesh of fruit, not the seeds, that is most highly valued. The light green-yellowish juice is tangy and mildly herbal in taste – a little like root beer – and can be flavoured with sour plums. The juice is also boiled with rock sugar to a syrup and used in a much sweeter, brownish iced drink.

YOGURT–BASED DRINKS

Yogurt-based drinks are not commonly found at restaurants, coffeeshops or hawker stalls. But at home, many drink fermented probiotic milk drinks, such as the Japanese brand Yakult and the locally produced version Vitagen, for their health benefits – both drinks are supposed to be good for your gut, aiding digestion. In high-rise residential areas of Singapore you may even catch sight of the Yakult lady, with her little trolley in tow, making weekly deliveries.

Lassi, an Indian yogurt drink, is mostly available at Indian coffeeshops and restaurants. It can be served plain, savoury (seasoned with a little salt, pepper and cumin) or sweet (flavoured with sugar, pureed mango or rose water).

BEER & other ALCOHOLIC DRINKS

Alcohol consumption in Malaysia, a Muslim majority nation, is low, while in Singapore high taxes on alcoholic drinks also keeps their consumption in check. But when locals do choose to imbibe, it's an ice-cold beer that is sure to hit the spot.

More often than not, Tiger and Anchor are the two local beer brands you get to choose from when you ask for beer in Malaysia or Singapore. Tiger is an easy-to-drink, smooth lager that goes well with local food. The brand was started in 1932 in Singapore as a joint venture with the Dutch Heineken brewery. Anchor is a pilsener beer that is crisp, refreshing and made with aromatic European hops for a rich, full-flavoured taste. Both are most readily available across both countries in restaurants and some coffeeshops.

CRAFT BEERS

One of the reasons for the lack of a range of beers in Malaysia is that the market is dominated by the products brewed by the multi-nationals Heineken and Carlsberg, and that the authorities are loath to grant more brewing licences. There are also very high taxes on all alcoholic drinks. However, in recent years, craft brewing is gaining a foothold. Napex Brewery, based in Port Klang, Selangor, brews Legend, a pale German-style lager; Legend Black, a black lager; and Jaz, another lager. In Kuala Lumpur you may also come across Modern Madness, a craft brewery turning out ales with local flavours such as lemongrass, chrysanthemum flowers and even the herbal pork soup *bak kut teh*!

In Singapore it's a very different story with the local microbrew industry coming of age, and more bars, cafes and restaurants jumping on the craft-brew bandwagon. Among the many local ales to search out are those produced by craft-brew pioneers Brewerkz and RedDot BrewHouse, both founded in the late 1990s; and LeVeL33, which bills itself as the 'World's Highest Urban Micro-brewery', housed in the Marina Bay Financial Centre building – here you can enjoy a blonde lager, an IPA and a stout while taking in amazing views of the Lion City.

WINE

Although grapes are grown in the more temperate uplands of Malaysia, the country's tropical climate plus Islam's prohibition on alcohol have mitigated against the founding of any local wine industry. However, in recent decades the market for imported wine (especially red wine) has grown dramatically in Malaysia and Singapore. Many restaurants (except for Malay Muslim establishments) have a modest wine list. Fine-dining Western restaurants and even some high-end Chinese restaurants carry extensive wine lists that cover both Old World and New World wines.

While the earlier wave of wine connoisseurs went for French wines in a big way, Australian and American wines and those of other New World wine regions are now just as popular. Many supermarkets now have wine sections, and wine stores are mushrooming in the larger cities – most notably in Kuala Lumpur and Singapore.

One locally produced wine you may come across is ReissJaden. This label makes fruit wine from Malaysian ingredients such as lemon, pineapple, ginger and coffee seeds. These wines contain no preservatives and no artificial flavouring or colouring agents.

TODDY (Palm-Sap Wine)

Toddy is a sweet, mildly alcoholic juice extracted from various palms, including coconut palms. The juice is tapped from the unopened flower of the fruit while it is still in its bud sheath. The juice drips into an earthen pot hung overnight, and in the morning, a toddy tapper climbs the palm to collect it. Toddy gets increasingly alcoholic as it ferments over time, and is most alcoholic 48 hours after it's drawn, when it's about as strong as a beer. Because of its association with the Indian Tamil and Keralan migrants who were brought by the British to labour in the peninsula's rubber plantations, toddy is considered a

Left: Toca Me Bar on Club Street, the heart of Singapore's booming bar scene
Right: Barrio Chino Bar on Club Street

'poor man's' drink. It is rarely found on cafe or bar menus beyond the more esoteric and adventurous establishments in Kuala Lumpur, Penang and Singapore.

TUAK (Rice Wine)

This is a potent rice wine, similar to Japanese sake, made by the tribal people of Borneo. *Tuak* is the word used for the drink in Sarawak (in Sabah, it is called *lihing*) and it is a deeply rooted tradition for the Dayak peoples of Borneo. This milky liquid tastes like a sweet, fruity white wine, and if visiting a longhouse, be prepared to down copious amounts of it: sustained consumption of *tuak*, by both hosts and visitors, is a major part of the local welcome.

SPIRITS

Locally distilled alcohols in Malaysia – such as *arak,* made from the juice of the coconut palm, and *samsu,* the cheapest type of white spirit – generally get a bad rap and should be avoided. However, in the trendier of Kuala Lumpur and Singapore cocktail bars you may come across some intriguing local spirits such as Timah, a double-peated blended whisky made by Winepak in Ipoh, which won a silver medal at the San Francisco 2020 world spirits competition.

SINGAPORE SLING

The Long Bar of the historic Raffles Hotel is where the iconic Singapore Sling cocktail was first mixed. History has it that Hainanese bartender Ngiam Tong Boon created the pink-hued, gin-based concoction in 1915 as something that women could drink without raising local eyebrows, because it appeared to be simply a mix of fruit juices.

PHRASES

English is widely spoken and understood across Malaysia and Singapore. But some Malay phrases will help you navigate a foodie exploration of the country.

The national language of Malaysia is Malay, also known as Bahasa Malaysia. It's spoken with slight variations throughout Malaysia and Singapore, although it's by no means the only language. As both are former British colonies, English is used and understood widely – though it often is spoken in a patois known as Manglish in Malaysia and Singlish in Singapore.

Various dialects of Chinese, including Hokkien and Cantonese, are spoken by those of Chinese ancestry. Mandarin is fairly widely used, too. Malaysians and Singaporeans of Indian ancestry will also speak Tamil, Malayalam, Hindi and other languages of the subcontinent.

In Singapore the official languages alongside Malay (which is mostly restricted to the Malay community there) are Tamil, Mandarin and English. Many different languages and dialects are spoken by the tribal people of Malaysian Borneo, but in general you'll get by very easily with English in this region, too.

In Bahasa Malaysia, most letters are pronounced more or less the same as their English counterparts – except for the letter 'c' which is always pronounced as the 'ch' in 'chair'. Nearly all syllables carry equal emphasis, but a good approximation is to lightly stress the second-to-last syllable.

Left: Eating out and shopping, two extremely popular pastimes

Useful Phrases

Do you speak English?
Andah anda berbahasa Inggeris?

Are you hungry?
Anda lapar?

I am hungry.
Saya lapar.

Have you eaten yet?
Sudah makan, belum?

I've already eaten.
Saya sudah makan.

Eating Out

... restaurant   restoran ...

Cantonese   Cina

Malay   Melayu

Indian   India

Peranakan   Baba

Japanese   Jepun

French   Perancis

Italian   Itali

Where's a ...?   ... di mana?

cheap restaurant
kedai makan murah

restaurant   kedai makan

hawker centre   pusat penjaja

Table for ..., please.
Ada meja untuk ..., orang.

Please join me.   Jemput makan.

Do you accept credit cards?
Sentuju dengan kad kredit?

THE MENU

Can I see the menu, please?
Minta senarai makanan?

Do you have a menu in English?
Ada sanarai makanan dalam
Inggris?

What are today's specials?
Apa istimewa hari ini?

MENU DECODER

Beef   Daging lembu

Chicken   Ayam

Lamb   Anak kambing

Mutton   Daging kambing

Pork   Daging babi

Fish   Ikan

Prawn   Udang

Seafood   Makanan laut

ORDERING

I'd like ...   Saya mau ...

I'd like the set lunch, please.
Saya mau makan tengah hari.

What's the soup of the day?
Apa kuah hari ini?

What's in this dish?
Ini termasuk apa?

Do you have sauce?
Ada kecap?

Not too spicy, please.
Kurang pedas.

Is that dish spicy?
Apakah makanan itu pedas?

I like it hot and spicy!
Saya suka pedas lagi!

YOU MAY HEAR

Anything else?   Ada lagi?

We have no ... today.
Hari ini tak ada ...

Enjoy your meal!
Selamat makan!

What would you like to drink?
Minum apa?

JUST TRY IT!

What's that/this?
Apa itu/ini?

What's the speciality here?
Apa keistimewaan di sini?

What do you recommend?
Anda menyaran apa?

What are they eating?
Mereka makan apa?

I'll try what they're having.
Saya mau percubaan seperti yang
mereka.

THROUGHOUT THE MEAL

What's in this dish?
Ini termasuk apa?

Not too spicy, please.
Kurang pedas.

Is that dish spicy?
Apakah makanan itu pedas?

I like it hot and spicy!
Saya suka pedas lagi!

It's not hot. (temperature)
Ini tak panas.

It's not hot. (spicy)
Ini tak pedas.

It's taking a long time, please hurry up.
Sudah lama, tolong lebih cepat.

Please bring me ...
Bisa minta ...

> **an ashtray**   tempat abu rokok
>
> **some/more bread**   roti lagi
>
> **a fork**   garpu
>
> **a glass**   gelas
>
> **a knife**   pisau
>
> **a napkin**   tisu
>
> **a plate**   piring
>
> **a spoon**   camca
>
> **a teaspoon**   camca the
>
> **a toothpick**   pencungkil gigi
>
> **rice**   nasi
>
> **salt**   garam
>
> **pepper**   lada
>
> **soy sauce**   kecap
>
> **water**   air minum

SOMETHING WRONG?

This food is ...   Makanan ini ...

> **cold**   sejuk
>
> **hot (temperature)**   panas
>
> **hot (spicy)**   pedas
>
> **delicious**   sedap
>
> **spoiled/stale**   basi
>
> **undercooked**   mentah
>
> **very oily**   berminyak

VEGETARIANS & VEGANS

I'm a vegetarian.
Saya hanya makan sayuran.

I'm a vegan, I don't eat meat or dairy products.
Saya tidak makan daging dan susu.

Is it cooked with pork lard or chicken stock?
Ini ada masak babi dan ayam?

I don't want any meat at all.
Saya tak mau daging.

Don't add egg.
Jangan pakai telur.

I don't eat ...   Saya tak makan ...

> **chicken/poultry**   ayam
>
> **meat**   daging
>
> **fish**   ikan

> **pork**   daging babi
>
> **seafood**   makanan laut
>
> **eggs**   telur

Do you have any vegetarian dishes?
Ada makanan nabati?

Can you recommend a vegetarian dish, please?
Dapatkan anda mengusulkan auatu makanan nabati apa?

Does this dish have meat?
Makanan ini ada dagingnya?

Can I get this without the meat?
Boleh tak masak tanpa daging?

Is the sauce meat-based?
Adakah kechap ini dari daging?

Does it contain eggs/dairy products?
Makanan ini ada telur/susu tak?

HALAL

Is this halal?
Adakah ini halal?

I'd like a halal meal.
Saya mahukan makanan yang halal.

INTOLERANCES & ALLERGIES

I'm allergic to ...
Saya tak boleh tahan makan ...

Is it ...?   Adakah ia ...?

gluten-free   Bebas gluten

lactose-free   Bebas laktosa

wheat-free   Bebas gandum

salt-free   Bebas garam

sugar-free   Bebas gula

yeast-free   Bebas ragi

CHILDREN

Are children allowed?
Anak-anak boleh masuk?

Is there a children's menu?
Ada seranai untuk bayi?

Do you have a highchair for the baby?
Ada kerusi untuk bayi?

ORDERING DRINKS

I'd like something to drink.
Saya mau minum.

Can I have a (beer), please?
Minta (bir), terimah kasih?

CHOOSING WINE

May I see the wine list, please?
Minta senarai air anggur?

What is a good year?
Apalah tahun banyak?

Can you recommend a good wine?
Andalah boleh menyaran air anggur yang baik?

May I taste it?
Say boleh rasa ini?

Please bring me another bottle.
Satu lagi botol, terima kasih.

I'd like a glass/bottle of ... wine.
Saya mau satu glas/botol ... air anggur.

red   merah

rosé   berwana merah

sparkling   berkilau-kiluan

white   putiho

This wine tastes great!
Sedap!

This wine has gone bad.
Ini air anggur tidak baik.

AT THE END OF THE MEAL

Thank you, that was delicious.
Sedap sekali, terima kasih.

The bill/check, please.
Minta bon.

Do you accept credit cards?
Sentuju dengan kad kredit?

At the Bar

Shall we go for a drink?
Mau pagi minum?

I'll buy you a drink.
Saya membelikan anda minuman.

Thanks, but I don't feel like it.
Terima kasih, tidak.

I don't drink (alcohol).
Saya tidak minum (minuman keras).

What would you like?
Anda mau minum apa?

You can get the next one.
Anda boleh bayar yang berikut.

It's on me Saya bayar.

It's my round.
Saya bayar kali ini.

Ok. Baik.

Can I buy you a coffee?
Saya membeli kopi untuk anda ya?

Cheers! Selamat!

No ice. Tidak air batu.

Can I have ice, please?
Minta air batu?

Is food available here?
Adalah makanan di sini?

I'm a bit tired. I'd better get home.
Saya penat. Pergi rumah dulu.

GETTING ATTENTION AT THE BAR

I'm next! Saya yang berikut!

Excuse me! Permisi!

I was here before this lady/ gentleman.
Saya menunggu lebih dulu daripada dia.

Same again, please.
Yang sama, terima kasih.

Drinks

I'll have ...   Saya mau minum ...

beer   bir

wine   wain

soft drink   minuman ringan

bottled water   air botol

citrus juice   air limau

water   air

milk   susu

coffee   kopi

tea   teh

Clockwise from top left: An outdoor bar in Singapore; A beach bar on the island of Langkawi; Green sago in coconut milk

171

shopping for food

Where is the nearest (market)?
Di mana (pasar) terdekat?

Where can I find the (sugar)?
(Gula) di mana?

I'm just looking.
Saya lihat lihat saja.

No!   Tidak!

Where can I buy ...?
Saya bisa membeli di mana ...?

This is a present for someone.
Hadiah ini untuk seseorang.

Can I taste it?   Boleh cicip?

Best before ...   Makan sebelum ...

Is this the best you have?
Apakah ini yang terbaik?

Do you have anything better?
Adalah yang lebih baik?

What's the local speciality?
Makanan khas daerah ini apa?

Can you give me a discount?
Boleh potongan harga?

BUYING THINGS

I am looking for ...
Saya mencari ...

Can I have a ...   Minta ...

    bottle   botol

    box   kotak

    can/tin   tin

    packet/sachet/bag   Paket

How much?   Berapa harga?

How much is (a kilo of cheese)?
Berapa harga (satu kilo kaju)?

How much (for) ...?
Berapa harga (untuk) ...?

    both   keduanya

    per fruit   satu buah

    per piece   satu bahagian

    this   ini

Do you have anything cheaper?
Adalah yang lebih murah?

Give me (half) a kilo, please.
Minta (setengah) kilo.

I'd like (six) ...   Saya mau (enam) ...

WHAT'S ON THE LIST?

I'd like to buy ...
Saya mau membeli ...

bread roti

butter mentega

cheese keju

eggs telur

flour tepung

fruit and vegetables
buah dan sayur

honey manisan

jam jem

margarine marjerin

milk susu

oil minyak

pepper lada

rice (uncooked) beras

salt garam

sugar gula

yogurt dadih

family meals

Let me help you.
Saya bisa menolong.

Can I watch you make this?
Saya boleh pemerhatian anda membuat ini?

You're a great cook!
Anda tukang masak yang baik!

This is brilliant! Sedap lagi!

Do you have the recipe for this?
Anda ada resipi untuk makanan ini?

Is this a family recipe?
Ini resipi makanan keluarga?

Are the ingredients local?
Ini bahannya dari daerah ini?

I've never eaten food like this before.
Saya belum pernah makan makanan ini.

Is this a vegetable?
Ini adakah sayur?

Is this a fruit? Ini adakah buah?

If you ever come to ... I'll cook you a local dish. Kalau nada ke ... saya masak makanan.

Could you pass the (salt) please?
Minta (garam).

One is enough, thank you.
Satu cukup, terima kasih.

Do you use ... in this?
Ada ... dalam masakan ini?

No thank you, I'm full.
Terima kasih, sudah kenyang.

Thanks very much for the meal.
Terima kasih banyak atas makanan.

I really appreciate it.
Saya sangat menghargai.

Left: Buying home-cooked dishes in a market in Kota Kinabalu
Right: Diwali decorations in Singapore's Little India

REGIONS

Different and similar. The people of Malaysia and Singapore are staunchly proud of their regional food. Sometimes the variation between the recipes of the same dish is very subtle while, in other cases, the cuisine is totally unique to a specific location.

Malaysia and Singapore have similar populations, share a tropical climate and were both in centuries past home to important trading ports along the Spice Route. As a result, their cuisines are characterised by comparable flavours and are built on a shared foundation of basic ingredients. Yet there are distinct regional differences – both between the same dishes cooked in Malaysia and Singapore and between the disparate Malaysian states.

The regional food variations are fascinating in the way they have been influenced by history more than geographical differences. By the 16th century the Malay Archipelago had, for hundreds of years, been part of a complex trading network stretching from Africa to China. This was already making an impact on the local dining habits and tastes, such as with Melaka's Peranakan (or Nonya) and Kristang cuisines which, respectively, fused Chinese and Portuguese styles of cooking with local ingredients. The 13 states and three federal territories of modern-day Malaysia mostly have their roots in the independently ruled, pre-colonial Malay kingdoms. In each there are both subtle and significant differences in the types of food served and the recipes that are passed down from generation to generation. The same goes for Singapore, an independent nation only since 1965.

Colonial patterns of migration have strongly shaped the dishes encountered throughout the west and south of Peninsula Malaysia. Chinese food, *mamak* (halal Indian) specialities, South Indian treats and Malay dishes jostle on the table alongside Peranakan delights. On the peninsula's east coast, the states of Kelantan and Terengganu were once considerably isolated from the rest of the country by the interior's jungles and mountains. They received few Chinese and Indian immigrants thus regional specialities have remained staunchly Malay. Meanwhile, in Malaysian Borneo, you can add to the culinary mix the foods of the tribal peoples of Sarawak and Sabah.

And if you're in need of a break from all these local cuisines, then look no farther than Singapore; the island nation's high-end dining scene is second to none in Southeast Asia. Whether you're hankering for handmade pasta, *steak frites*, super-fresh sashimi or a molecular gastronomic morsel quick-frozen in liquid nitrogen and bedecked with foam, you'll find it in a posh restaurant here.

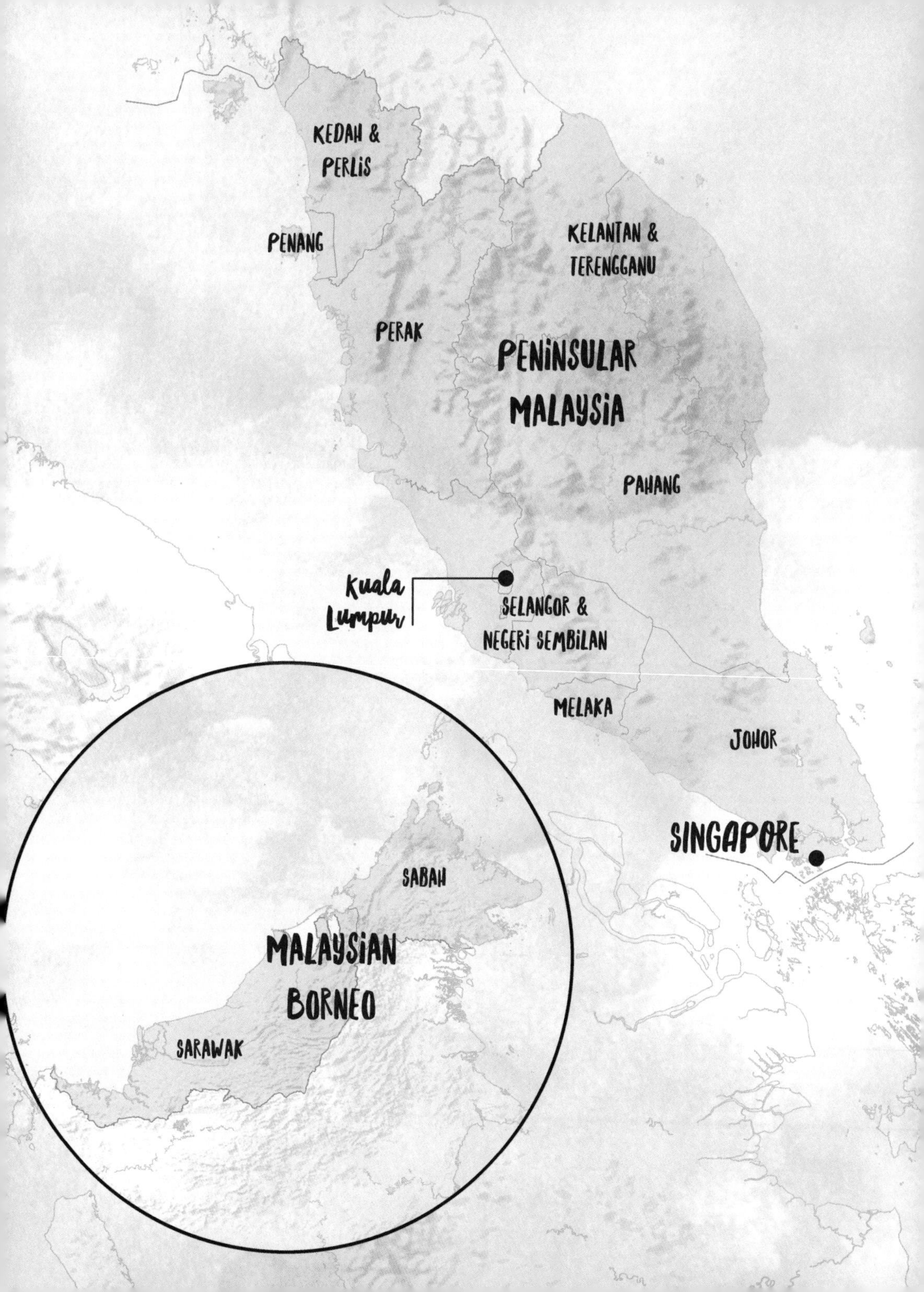

KEDAH &
PERLIS

PENANG

KELANTAN &
TERENGGANU

PERAK

PENINSULAR
MALAYSIA

PAHANG

Kuala
Lumpur

SELANGOR &
NEGERI SEMBILAN

MELAKA

JOHOR

SINGAPORE

SABAH

MALAYSIAN
BORNEO

SARAWAK

PERLIS & KEDAH

These two states, on the northwest coast of Peninsular Malaysia, are considered the rice bowls of Malaysia. They produce over half of the country's domestic rice supply and are covered with lustrous paddy fields.

THAI INFLUENCE

Historically, these states have close associations with Thailand, and were only relinquished from Siamese control under the 1909 Anglo-Siamese Treaty which established the modern border between Thailand and Malaysia. Centuries of Thai cultural influence and settlement have created a local preference for hot, spicy flavours paired with sour accents. Lemongrass, kaffir lime leaves, lime juice and fish sauce are more common in kitchens here. Stalls selling *tom yam* (spicy and sour Thai seafood soup) line the streets of Padang Besar, the border town to Thailand. The version served here has a clear soup, misleading you into thinking it isn't at all spicy.

Locals insist that Kedah laksa differs from its similarly sour and spicy counterpart, Penang laksa (also known as *asam laksa*). The traditional Kedah laksa uses tamarind in dried slices and eel rather than the mackerel or sardine flakes found in Penang laksa. What is consistent, however, is the fact that both use rice noodles. In Kedah and Perlis, a helping of *otak udang* (prawn sauce) tempers the sourness of the dish and shares centre stage with a garnish of shredded cucumber, onions, torch ginger bud, chilli and mixed herbs.

MORE MALAY

In contrast to the other states along the west coast, the cuisine of Perlis and Kedah remains more staunchly Malay, possibly because both states remain strongly Islamic. The region, populated by

Don't Miss

 Laksa Kedah Also known as *laksa utara*, this is a spicy and intensely fish-flavoured version of the ubiquitous, soupy noodle dish.
 Tom yam Sour, spicy Thai seafood soup popular along the border between Perlis and Thailand.
 Gulai nangka *Nangka* (jackfruit) is a major crop in Kedah, and forms the basis of this curry.
 Pulut Glutinous rice which is paired with fruits such as mango, durian and banana.
 Kuih serabai Rice-flour pancakes dipped in a syrup made of coconut milk and palm sugar.
 Nasi ulam A rice salad of finely shredded tropical herbs and vegetables, aromatic spices and toasted grated coconut.

Above: Limestone hills overlook rice paddies in Perlis

rice farmers and fishermen, focuses on simple food such as *ikan bakar* (grilled fish), *kanji Kedah* (rice porridge with chicken or beef and prawns, and flavoured with ginger, lemongrass and fenugreek) and *ketupat pulut* (glutinous rice half-cooked in coconut milk, rolled into tubes, steamed in banana leaves and served with *serunding daging*, spicy, dry shredded beef).

Coconut features in several local recipes, such as the sweet snack *kuih dangai*, the green glutinous-rice dish *emping*, and *pulut ikan kering*, a simple and traditional Perlis breakfast of glutinous rice, fried or dried fish and grated coconut. Also keep an eye out at markets for the *mempelam harum manis,* local seasonal mangoes that are intensely sweet and beautifully fragrant.

DELICIOUS SEAFOOD

Kedah and Perlis are also famous for their seafood. *Ikan bakar* (grilled fish) is ubiquitous at night markets and food stalls, with choices including *ikan terubuk* (toli shad), *kembung* (Indian mackerel), *pari* (stingray) and *keli* (catfish). They are usually marinated in spices. Also on offer will be crabs, grilled squid or prawns.

Salted fish and fish crackers are a delicacy in this region, too, along with fish prepared in according to the *pekasam* method. After sitting in salt for a few days, the fish is washed thoroughly, mixed with fried dry rice, tamarind juice and brown sugar and left to ferment in an airtight container for about two weeks. This method of preservation keeps the fish edible for months, even if kept outside the fridge.

LANGKAWI'S ROVING NIGHT MARKET

Fans of Malay eats visiting Langkawi shouldn't miss the rotating pasar malam (night market), held at various points across the island. It's a great chance to indulge in cheap, take-home meals and snacks, and is held from about 6pm to 10pm at the following locations:

Mon *Jalan Makam Mahsuri Lama, in the centre of the island, not far from MARDI Agro Technology Park.*

Tue *Kedawang, just east of the airport.*

Wed & Sat *Kuah, opposite Masjid Al-Hana; this is the largest market.*

Thu *Bohor Tempoyak, at the northern end of Pantai Cenang.*

Fri *Padang Lalang, at the roundabout near Pantai Pasir Hitam.*

Sun *Padang Matsirat, near the roundabout just north of the airport.*

PENANG

Offering up some of Malaysia's best multiculinary cooking, Penang is generally regarded as the region's gastronomic ground zero. Kuala Lumpur residents have been known to make the four-hour drive to Penang for a single meal, and hungry Singaporeans pack out hotels on weekends.

BETELNUT ISLAND

While most people know of Penang as the pearl-shaped island off the northwest coast of Peninsular Malaysia, Penang State also covers the mainland port town of Butterworth and the surrounding area of Seberang Perai. Chinese seafarers were aware of the island, which they called Pulau Pinang (Betelnut Island), as far back as the 15th century, but it was little more than a way station en route to trading ports. It wasn't until the early 1700s that colonists arrived from Sumatra and established settlements at Batu Uban and the area now covered by southern George Town, Penang's capital.

The island came under the control of the sultan of Kedah, but in 1771 the sultan signed the first agreement with the British East India Company, handing them trading rights in exchange for military assistance against Siam (present-day Thailand). In 1786 Captain Francis Light, on behalf of the East India Company, took formal possession of Penang, hoisting the Union Flag above Britain's first Malay (and Southeast Asian) territory.

Light permitted new arrivals to claim as much land as they could clear and, together with a duty-free port and an atmosphere of liberal tolerance, this quickly attracted settlers from all over Asia. By the 19th century Penang was considered one of the finest islands in the world for nutmeg and cloves. The growth of the city's spice trade was accompanied by the arrival of immigrants: Malays from Kedah, Chinese from Canton, Achehnese from Sumatra, Indians from British India, Thais from across the border and Burmese. The food of Penang reflects the intermingling of these cultures and is a gastronomic highlight of Malaysia.

NONYA CUISINE

Penang's Peranakan community has its roots in the intermarriage of early Chinese migrants with local women. Because of Penang's

THE FOOD OF PENANG reflects the intermingling of CULTURES AND IS A gastronomic HIGHLIGHT OF MALAYSIA

geographical location, Peranakan cuisine (also referred to
as Nonya cuisine) here is heavily influenced by punchy Thai
flavours. Chillies, lime juice and tamarind pulp are frequently
used to create distinctly sour, lip-numbingly hot sensations.
The classic example of this is Penang's version of the noodle
dish laksa, commonly known as *asam laksa* after the tart
asam (tamarind) that is one of its key ingredients. The dish
is made from rice noodles topped with a spicy and sour
fish gravy, flakes of fish (usually mackerel or sardine, but
sometimes skipjack tuna) and garnished with slivers of fresh
pineapple, cucumber, chilli, mint and finely shredded torch
ginger flowers. An optional splash of *heh ko* (dark shrimp
sauce) provides an added flavour kick.

There are also differences in the way certain Peranakan
dishes are cooked, such as with the spicy fish paste *otak
otak*. The classic Penang *otak otak* has the addition of betel
leaves to its recipe and is wrapped in banana leaves before
being steam-cooked. This gives the dish a soft texture and
a milder taste than the Melaka version, which is grilled over
charcoal and thus has a strong smoky smell and flavour as
well as a firmer texture.

Other Peranakan dishes to look out for include *jiu hoo
char* (stir-fried shredded cuttlefish with yam bean) and
popiah, a type of non-fried spring roll that was brought
to Penang by Hokkien and Teochew migrants during the
British colonial period.

THE INDIAN INFLUENCE

The first Indians on Penang arrived as soldiers and sailors
with Captain Light. With them they brought their spicy
cooking traditions and tastes. The popular Penang meal
nasi kandar (steamed rice served with a variety of curries
and side dishes) has its origins in the Indian food hawkers
who would carry around their buckets of rice and curry
balanced at either end of a *kandar* (pole).

Another Indian Penang speciality is *pasembur*, a
salad which is known as *rojak* in other parts of Malaysia

and Singapore. The Penang version mixes up pieces of fried tofu, boiled egg, shredded cucumber, jicama (a type of turnip), prawn crackers and a selection of fried seafood, all topped with a thick and creamy sauce made from tomato, peanuts and sweet potato. In hawker centres, look out, too, for *murtabak* (pan-fried dough folded around minced or diced chicken, beef or mutton, or vegetables).

KING OF FRUITS

Penang's highlands have been cultivated for fruit crops, such as nutmeg, for centuries. But it's the island's durian orchards, many of which were only planted in the mid-20th century, that have become renowned for the quality of their pungent fruits. From across the region, durian lovers flock to Penang in June and July for the main harvesting season, when the ripe, spike-encrusted fruits begin to drop from the trees. There are dozens of different varieties to sample, including local favourite Red Prawn, so-called because this durian's flesh has a pink, cooked-prawn appearance.

PENANG PICKLES

At George Town's Chowrasta Market you can sample the region's best jeruk *(sweet and sour pickled fruits), a Penang delicacy. Among the locally grown preserved fruits on sale are familiar ones such as nutmeg, papaya, guava, mango and banana, as well as less familiar ones like salak (snakeskin fruit), kedondong (great hog plum) and cermai (a type of gooseberry). The fruits are sliced, soaked in brine, drained and rinsed before being soaked in syrup. The amount of brine and syrup used differs from stall to stall so ask to sample before you buy – some pickles are sweeter while other are more sour.*

Left: *Tau sar piah,* pastries filled with red-bean paste

From left: *Pasembur (rojak)* at Gurney Drive hawker stalls; A Chinese tea stall in George Town

HAWKER-STALL HEAVEN

Not eating at a hawker stall in George Town is like skipping the Louvre in Paris – unthinkable! There are scores of hawker centres and stalls in and around town, from shophouse-bound *kopitiam* (coffeeshops) to open-air markets made up of mobile stalls.

Keep in mind that hawker-stall vendors run flexible schedules, so don't be surprised if one isn't there during your visit. A good strategy is to avoid Mondays and Thursdays, when many vendors tend to stay at home. Top picks include the following:

GURNEY DRIVE HAWKER STALLS

One of Penang's most famous hawker complexes sits amid high-rise buildings bordered by the sea, about 3km (2 miles) west of George Town. Tourists and locals rush in for an almost overwhelming selection of Muslim and Chinese-Malay dishes.

LORONG BARU (NEW LANE) HAWKER STALLS

Ask locals where their favourite hawker stalls are, and they'll generally mention this night-time street extravaganza, located about 1km (0.6 miles) west of George Town city centre. Prepare to battle for a spot if you're visiting at the weekend.

PULAU TIKUS HAWKER CENTRE

Before those bland guesthouse breakfasts get you down, consider a visit to this busy morning market area. The market is about 2.5km (1.5 miles) north of the centre of George Town.

→ **Asam laksa** Rice noodles in a spicy, sour fish gravy, topped with flakes of mackerel, pineapple and fragrant herbs.

→ **Perut ikan** A Nonya dish of salted and preserved fish innards cooked in a coconut curry flavoured with mint and dressed with sliced beans and pineapple.

→ **Char kway teow** Broad, flat rice-flour noodles stir-fried with Chinese sausage and egg, topped with shrimp.

→ **Pong piah** Hokkien flaky puff pastry filled with white molasses. Variations include *tau sar piah* (filled with red-bean paste) and *tambun piah* (with yellow-lentil paste)

→ **Jus pala** Tangy juice made from nutmegs, grown on the island, and often flavoured with sour plums.

→ **Pasembur** A salad of cucumber, potatoes, soft tofu, turnip, bean sprouts, prawn fritters and seafood doused in a sweet, sour and nutty sauce.

SEA PEARL LAGOON CAFE

The excellent seafood and unique location of this basic hawker centre – seemingly hidden in a Chinese temple complex looking out over the North Channel – make the Sea Pearl one of our favourite places to eat outside the city centre. It's 7km (4.3 miles) northwest of George Town.

MEDAN RENONG PADANG KOTA LAMA

One side of this seaside food centre, a short walk from George Town's Padang, is called 'Islam' and serves halal Malay food, and the other is called 'Cina' and serves Chinese and Malay specialities, including the absolutely delicious *rojak* at the stall 101 Rojak.

LEBUH PRESGRAVE HAWKER STALLS

A famous vendor of *Hokkien mee* (yellow noodles fried with sliced meat, boiled squid, prawns and strips of fried egg) draws most folks to this open-air hawker congregation, in easy walking distance from central George Town.

PERAK

While the state capital, Ipoh, has an outstanding reputation as a food city, it's not the only place in Perak to find delicious food. There's Kuala Kangsar's take on laksa, plus cooling, sweet *cendol* in Taiping and fresh seafood by the coast.

IPOH SPECIALITIES

Ipoh lies at the heart of Kinta Valley, once the world's richest tin-producing field. During the 18th and 19th centuries, tin mining lured Chinese, Indian, Malay and European fortune-seekers to Ipoh, making it one of British Malaya's richest towns. Everyone brought their various food cultures with them, and none more so than the Cantonese and Hakka settlers whose descendants run many of the wonderful places to eat clustered in Ipoh's old town.

Locals believe that deposits from the rich karst formations around Ipoh seep into the groundwater, giving the city's food a special quality. The city has a number of signature dishes but its most famous by far is *tauge ayam*: tender poached chicken served with Ipoh's fat bean sprouts and rice, the latter cooked in chicken broth, or a bowl of rice noodles. There are many places to eat this, but locals swear by the restaurant Cowan Street on the corner of Jln Raja Ekram and Jln Sultan Abdul. There are no prizes for guessing what the signature dish is at Famous Hakka Mee: the eponymous *hakka mee* wheat noodles, topped with salty ground pork and served with a side bowl of broth with fish and pork balls and tofu. *Kopi putih*, known as Ipoh white coffee and famous across Malaysia, uses a method of roasting beans with palm-oil margarine that was allegedly invented at the *kopitiam* Sin Yoon Loong, where you can also sample luscious *chee cheong fun* (flat rice noodles with soy sauce, shrimp and spice). Foodies also make a beeline to the legendary Ipoh stall Funny Mountain Soya Bean, which has been serving *tau fu fah*, a fresh, warm and silky bean-curd pudding, since 1952.

FERMENTED DURIAN

To make the fermented salted durian dish *tempoyak*, locals scrape the pungent fruit's flesh off its seeds, mix it with salt and leave it in an airtight jar in the fridge for at least three days. The resulting strongly flavoured ingredient is a key component of the curried fish dish *gulai ikan masak tempoyak*.

RENDANG TOK

The beef and curry stew *rendang tok* is distinguished by its liberal use of spices, as well as aromatics such as lemongrass and *cekur* root. The original recipe is said to hail from the kitchens of the royal palace in Kuala Kangsar and is distinguished by its drier texture and darker colour, with the beef fried in the rendered fat.

Kuala Kangsar's traditional laksa uses wheat rather than rice noodles and the dish's tamarind and sardine gravy is lighter in body.

STREET FOOD IN TAIPING

Taiping, Perak's second largest town and one of the rainiest places in Peninsular Malaysia, is hot on the heels of foodie favourites Penang and Ipoh with its street-food culture. Head to the Larut Matang Food Court to dig in to the local version of *char kway teow* (flat noodles garnished with fish balls the size of eyeballs) as well as other dishes such as *popiah* (fat rolls of crisp veggies wrapped in a wheat pancake). Ansari and Bismillah are two rival stalls that have been churning out the creamy, sweet, shaved-ice dessert *cendol* for decades.

Don't Miss

➔ **Tauge ayam** Tender poached chicken served with fresh bean sprouts and rice cooked in chicken broth.
➔ **Tempoyak** Fermented salted durian, mixed with pounded chilli to make a *sambal* and eaten with rice.
➔ **Ipoh kway teow** Thin rice noodles topped with a savoury sauce and shredded steamed chicken (and sometimes, slivers of Chinese mushroom).

➔ **Rendang tok** A rich, spicy stew of meltingly tender beef, often served at festive celebrations with *nasi himpit* (compressed rice cakes).
➔ **Ipoh curry laksa** Multicultural laksa with Indian curry leaves and a topping of Chinese barbecued roast pork.
➔ **Lemang** Glutinous rice mixed with coconut milk and salt, stuffed in a bamboo tube and cooked over a slow fire.

KUALA LUMPUR

KL is a nonstop feast. You can dine at elegant white-tablecloth restaurants or mingle with locals at street stalls, taking your pick from a global array of cuisines. Ingredients are fresh, cooking is high-quality and hygiene standards are excellent.

Founded in the mid-19th century, Kuala Lumpur (commonly known as KL) has grown from a wild and dangerous tin-mining settlement into an affluent modern Asian capital offering practically every type of food and drink you might desire. KL's culinary strengths lie in its gathering together of the major cuisines of the Malays, Chinese and Indians, who dominate the population, and the food preferences inherited during British colonial rule. Savour Kedah laksa along one street, then tuck into Penang *asam laksa* along another. Diversity also stretches to the style of dining available: you may choose to dress up and sample modern French creations with a Japanese twist one evening and go casual the next, when you eat standing on the kerb by a satay stall on wheels.

CHINESE CUISINE

Thanks to generations of immigrants from all parts of China, KL boasts a notable range of regional Chinese cuisines including Cantonese, Sichuanese, Teochew, Hokkien and Hakka. The city is famous for chilli *pan mee*. Literally 'board noodles', these hand-cut or hand-torn wheat noodles are tossed with dark soy sauce and garlic oil, garnished with chopped pork and crispy *ikan bilis* (dried anchovies), and served with soup on the side. Some versions include a poached egg.

INDIAN CUISINE

KL's two Little Indias – the official one in Brickfields and the other around Masjid India – are the places to sample the many delights of the Indian table, although you'll find the cuisine of the subcontinent served right across the city.

A very KL experience is a late night supper at a Muslim Indian-Malay eatery known as a *mamak*; these typically run 24 hours, serve comfort-food dishes such as *roti canai* (flaky flat bread), *mee goreng* (fried noodles) and *murtabak* (roti stuffed with meat). One of the city's most famous *mamaks* is Nasi Kandar Pelita on Jln Ampang.

BRITISH COLONIAL CUISINE

Dine at enough KL *kopitiam* (coffeeshops) and you're bound to run into lamb chops and mushroom soup. Though they may seem out of place on a menu that also features *belacan*, fried rice and fish in sour curry, these dishes are as much a part of the Malaysian culinary universe as *laksa lemak* (curry laksa). Introduced by the British but popularised in the

Right: Street eats at a KL night market
Over page: Jln Alor restaurant strip

early decades of the 20th century by the Hainanese immigrants who served as their private cooks – and who later became known for their prowess in the kitchen – Western classics such as chops (pork and chicken, in addition to lamb) and fish and chips are Malaysia's intergenerational comfort foods. Among the classic purveyors of this type of food is the Coliseum Café, famous for its sizzling steaks; and Yut Kee, known for its roast pork and *roti babi* (French toast stuffed with pork).

Don't Miss

● **Nasi lemak** Rice steamed in coconut milk and served with *ikan bilis* (small, dried sardines or anchovies), fried peanuts, half a hard-boiled egg, *sambal* (chilli sauce) and a selection of curries.

● **Roti canai** Flaky unleavened bread griddled with *ghee* until crisp and eaten with curry or *daal*; it's a breakfast favourite.

● **Maggi mee goreng** Just the KL speciality to hit the spot after a night of partying: fried instant noodles topped with an egg fried sunny-side up.

● **Laksa lemak** Also known as curry laksa, these noodles have a generous dosing of coconut milk and curried chicken. Mung-bean sprouts and deep-fried bean curd further fortify the dish.

● **Satay** Marinated chunks of chicken, beef or mutton, grilled over charcoal and served with a spicy peanut sauce, diced cucumber and pressed steamed rice.

BUNN CHOON TARTS

When in KL's Chinatown, it's all but obligatory to sample a sweet egg tart still warm from the oven at Bunn Choon. Fourth-generation owner-baker Wong Kok Tong and his wife use the family's original egg tart recipe, but they have also branched out to create charcoal black sesame and green tea versions. Tarts are available from 10.30am and tend to sell out quickly. They also serve various types of dim sum and other freshly baked pastries such as pineapple jam tarts and char siew sou (barbecue pork pastries).

KL DINING DISTRICTS

BUKIT BINTANG & KLCC

The mega malls of these glitzy districts, including Pavilion KL, Suria KLCC, Starhill Gallery and Lot 10, offer such a wide and top-quality range (from food courts to fine dining) that only the pickiest diner could find fault. A number of Bukit Bintang's best eateries are located along Tengkat Tong Shin, Jln Mesui and the ever-reliable Jln Alor. You'll also find some of the city's top fine-dining restaurants in these districts, including Dewakan, serving nouvelle Malay cuisine; and Nadodi, doing amazing takes on Indian fare.

PUDU

Not to be missed for a local breakfast are the stalls at Imbi Market at ICC Pudu. Top eats here include rice-flour noodles at Ah Fook Chee Cheong Fun and rice with rich, spicy *sambal* and myriad accompaniments at Ann Nasi Lemak. In the evening, Pudu's superior hawker-stall alley Glutton Street offers addictive fried chicken, *chai tow kway* (radish cake stir-fried with soy sauce, bean sprouts and egg), prawn fritters and barbecued dried squid, all for bargain prices.

CHINATOWN

Chinatown has some of the best and most inexpensive street food in KL. From breakfasts of *yong tau fu* (bean curd and vegetables stuffed with fish paste) and curry noodles on Madras Lane to a supper of satay and fried fish with an ice-cold beer at the popular open-air cafes along Jln Hang Lekir, you can hardly go wrong.

THE LAKE GARDENS

Officially named Tun Abdul Razak Heritage Park, KL's Lake

JALAN ALOR

The roadside restaurants and stalls lining Jln Alor are the great common denominator of KL's food scene, hauling in everyone from sequinned society babes to penny-strapped backpackers. From around 5pm till late every evening, the street transforms into a continuous open-air dining space, with hundreds of plastic tables and chairs and rival caterers shouting out to passers-by to drum up business (avoid the pushiest ones!). Most places serve alcohol and you can sample pretty much every Malay Chinese dish imaginable, from gai lan (Chinese greens) in oyster sauce to fried noodles with frogs' legs. Thai food is also popular. At Jln Alor's southern end, Wong Ah Wah is unbeatable for addictive spicy chicken wings, as well as grilled seafood and satay.

Gardens are home to Rebung, one of the city's best Malaysian dining experiences. The seemingly endless buffet spread is splendid, with all kinds of dishes that you'd typically only be served in a Malay home. Go hungry and book ahead at weekends, when it's super-busy. Also search out Tugu Café, a rustic food court outside the Civil Servants Club House (PPTD) that is rightly famed for its superb fish-head curry, deep-fried free-range chicken and banana fritters.

BRICKFIELDS

As KL's official 'Little India', Brickfields is home to some of the city's best Indian eateries, including many street stalls. The family who run Ammars, a stand in a parking lot across the road from KL Sentral, use giant woks to fry up tasty Indian snacks such as lentil *vadai* (fritters) flavoured with fennel seeds. Or head to low-key Lawanaya Food Corner on Lg Scott, a simple joint with a few tables lined up under a sheet of corrugated iron, where the same family has been preparing delicious curries for more than 30 years.

BANGSAR

Bangsar's brilliant range of dining options are concentrated in Bangsar Baru, in and around the Bangsar Village shopping malls. The Sunday-night Bangsar *pasar malam* (night market), held in the parking lot opposite the mosque on Jln Telawi 1, is an institution, while those in the know frequent Lucky Gardens and the collection of eateries hidden away on Lg Kurau.

CHOW KIT, MASJID INDIA & KAMPUNG BARU

During the day authentic hawker food is found around and inside Bazaar Baru Chow Kit; the atmosphere is lively, the food tasty and cheap, and you can pick up an astonishing variety of tropical fruit for dessert in the market. On Saturday the Masjid India *pasar malam* (night market) fills Lg Tuanku Abdul Rahman. Amid the headscarf and T-shirt sellers are plenty of stalls serving excellent Malay, Indian and Chinese snacks and colourful soya- and fruit-based drinks. Kampung Baru is great for Malay and Indonesian cheap eats at neighbourhood restaurants that stay open until the early hours.

Left: Selangor's famous Batu Caves are guarded by Hindu deity Lord Murugan

SELANGOR & NEGERI SEMBILAN

Minangkabau culture has injected eye-stinging bird's eye chilli and creamy coconut into Negeri Sembilan's cuisine, which includes such classics as *rendang.* The Selangor port of Klang is famed for its *bak kut teh* pork stew and its scintillating variety of Indian cuisine.

SELANGOR SPECIALITIES

From the sweet strawberries that thrive in the cooler climate of the Genting Highlands to the seafood fished along the Strait of Melaka coast, Selangor offers a broad range of edible delights. The state surrounds the federal territory of Kuala Lumpur and shares with it the same multicultural mix.

The port of Klang is famous for its renditions of the Chinese pork dish *bak kut teh.* Translating literally from Hokkien as 'meat bone tea', *bak kut teh* is made from pork ribs simmered in a complex, spicy broth that may also include offal, mushrooms and tofu. This fat-rich dish is typically eaten for breakfast or lunch. Also while here enjoy superior banana-leaf curry meals and authentic Indian snacks in Klang's Little India.

Kajang is known for its satay, so much so that *sate kajang* has become a generic name for satay where the meat chunks are bigger than normal and the sweet peanut sauce is served along with fried chilli paste. Stalls in Kajang also offer a wider selection, including venison, rabbit and fish, as well as offal such as gizzard and liver.

SUMATRAN INFLUENCE

During the 15th century, many Minangkabau people from Sumatra settled in the area that is now Negeri Sembilan. Most Minangkabau dishes are flavoured with a generous helping of *cili padi* (bird's eye chilli), creating a searingly spicy kick. Minangkabau *rendang* is time-consuming to prepare, but is considered to be unsurpassed in flavour. It is traditionally eaten with delicately salty yet sweet *lemang,* glutinous rice flavoured with coconut milk and cooked over a fire in bamboo poles lined with banana leaves.

Don't Miss

➔ **Apam johol** A fluffy steamed cake made with rice flour, yeast, coconut milk and brown sugar.
➔ **Bak kut teh** Pork stewed in a fragrant broth of star anise, ginseng, orange peel and other spices.
➔ **Masak lemak cili padi** Chicken, fish or seafood and vegetables poached in coconut milk blended with turmeric and ground *cili padi.*
➔ **Pekal** Traditional Javanese salad of raw vegetables served with a spicy peanut dressing.
➔ **Asam pedas udang galah** Giant freshwater prawns in a spicy-sour stew, a speciality of the Selangor town of Kuala Kubu Bharu.

MELAKA

Right: Melaka's riverfront

Melaka is the birthplace of Peranakan cooking, a fusion of Chinese and Malay cooking styles and ingredients. But this cuisine is just the start of the many types of speciality dishes, both traditional and more contemporary, available in this most ancient of Malay cities.

In the 15th century, Melaka was one of Southeast Asia's greatest trading ports. Over time it lost favour to Singapore, but this slowdown in trade protected much of the ancient architecture of the state capital, Melaka City, from falling foul of development. Visitors can now enjoy the city's Unesco-protected heritage areas alongside a renowned food scene that features Peranakan (also known as Nonya) and Portuguese Eurasian specialities.

MORE COCONUT

Unlike Penang's Peranakan community, who tend to favour sourer flavours (due in no small part to their proximity to Thailand), Melaka's Peranakans have a Malay-influenced penchant for coconut milk, chillies and fragrant roots. Hence their curries and other dishes are generally richer and creamier due to the amount of coconut milk they include – a good example being Melaka laksa.

SATAY & CHICKEN RICE

Melaka is also famous for unique spins on dishes you'll commonly find across Malaysia and Singapore. *Satay celup* (steamboat satay) is said to have been invented here in the 1950s at Capital Satay. Diners self-cook skewers of meat, seafood, vegetables, fish balls and hard-boiled quail eggs in a pot of bubbling sauce at their table, like an Asian version of fondue. The sauce includes peanuts, dried chilli, onion, garlic, lemongrass, brown sugar, turmeric, galangal and sesame seeds among other ingredients.

The local version of Hainanese chicken rice sees the grain cooked with chicken stock flavoured with garlic, ginger and spring onion, then rolled by hand while it is still hot to create firm balls of sticky savoury rice to be enjoyed with the poached meat.

Don't Miss

- ➡ **Chicken-rice balls** Steamed chicken paired with small balls of glutinous rice, often greased with stock or fat and served with a piquant dipping sauce.
- ➡ **Nonya laksa** Melaka's version of this coconut milk and noodle soup, infused with a powerful lemongrass flavour.
- ➡ **Curry debal** Fiery chicken curry that marries Portuguese and Malay flavours.
- ➡ **Satay celup** Skewers of tofu, fish or meat cooked in a spicy, bubbling soup, then dipped in a satay sauce.
- ➡ **Cendol** An addictive shaved-ice dessert with pandan green noodles, syrups, fruit and coconut milk.
- ➡ **Gula melaka** A caramel-like brown sugar extracted from the sugar palm, boiled and allowed to solidify in the hollows of bamboo poles.

KRISTANG CUISINE

Born of the marriage between Portuguese and local cooking cultures, Kristang cuisine is a mash-up of Peranakan-like dishes, Indian flavours, Chinese cooking styles and Malay spices. The west-European influence is most clearly seen in the cuisine's cakes and pastries. Apart from the very common *curry debal* (devil curry), a vinegary, spicy curry that originated in Goa, other Kristang dishes you may come across include *seybah* (braised meat served on a bed of salad, cucumber slices, dried tofu and vinegar-chilli sauce), *grago pikadel* (deep-fried krill balls) and *seccu* (dry beef curry).

JONKERS WALK NIGHT MARKET

Melaka City's weekly Jonkers Walk night market is a great opportunity to graze on local street foods while souvenir shopping, having your fortune told and listening to karaoke performances. This Chinatown street closes to traffic, shops stay open late and a party atmosphere prevails. Snack on the following:

Kuih nonya Coconut-milk and sticky-rice sweets, too colourful to resist.
Dodol Jellies made from the seaweed *agar-agar* in *gula melaka,* pandan and durian flavours.
Fried quail eggs A skewer of little eggs, laden with curry or sweetcorn, cooked on a griddle.
Pineapple tarts Buttery pastries with a chewy jam filling.
Popiah Spring rolls stuffed with shredded veggies, prawns, garlic and more.
Otak otak Spicy fish paste wrapped in banana leaves and grilled.

JOHOR

Ruled by a sultan since the early 16th century, Johor continues to nurture a strong Malay culture and cuisine. Even so, the foods of the southernmost state of Peninsular Malaysia are the result of centuries of international trade and cultural exchange.

PASTA NOT NOODLES

It was during a visit to Europe in 1866 that Johor's Sultan Abu Bakar apparently acquired a taste for pasta. On his return he instructed his royal chefs to use spaghetti instead of traditional rice noodles in his laksa – thus Johor laksa was born. This being a dish fit for a sultan, the thick, curry-like gravy is made of ground fish (most commonly wolf herring), coconut milk, dried shrimps, the sour fruit *asam gelugur* and a blend of herbs and spices including lemongrass and galangal. It is garnished with slices of onion, bean sprouts, mint leaves, *daun kesum* (Vietnamese coriander), julienned cucumber and white radish.

MUAR & JB SPECIALITIES

The coastal town of Muar is famous for its version of the mildly spicy fish mousse *otak otak* and as the birthplace of *mee bandung*, a bowl of yellow noodles and egg in a spicy shrimp and beef sauce.

Johor Bahru (JB), the state capital, is linked to Singapore by two causeways, which draw the two cities together both physically and gastronomically. In JB, as in Singapore, it's not hard to find prime samples of the flat-noodle dish *char kway teow* and the Indian Malay rice dish *nasi biryani* as well as newer inventions such as *murtabak* cheese, a *roti* parcel stuffed with meat and slices of melted cheese.

Don't Miss

- ➲ **Johor laksa** The main twist on this version of the noodle dish is the use of spaghetti rather than rice noodles and a very rich fish-and-coconut gravy.
- ➲ **Mee bandung** Noodles served in a spicy sauce of shrimp, onion, beef and egg.
- ➲ **Asam pedas** Tamarind-based red fish curry garnished with ladies' fingers (okra), tomatoes and *brinjal* (eggplant).
- ➲ **Pajeri nenas** Pineapple braised in a concoction of spices, coconut milk and palm sugar. Usually served as an accompaniment to rich rice dishes such as *nasi biryani*.
- ➲ **Satay Johor** Skewers of meat basted with a mixture of coconut milk and oil, brushed on with lemongrass stalks. This process is repeated as the meat cooks, giving it a delicate lemongrass flavour.

PAHANG

Right: Pahang's Cameron Highlands produce outstanding tea leaves

If you like fish, you'll love the cuisine of Pahang. From the ocean, there's an abundance of seafood; from the state's rivers and lakes comes silver catfish, locally known as *ikan patin* and cooked in a myriad of ways.

MALAYSIA'S LARGEST STATE

The old Pahang sultanate, centred in modern-day Pekan, was established in the 15th century. It was in the royal household that dishes such as *puding diraja* (literally 'royal pudding') were created. Pahang's interior was the preserve of the native Orang Asli tribes until prospectors started to arrive in the late 19th century when rich deposits of tin and gold were discovered. However, even then, the thick forest, network of rivers, valleys and mountain ridges made many locations impenetrable. This physical barrier is one reason why the cuisines of the east and west coasts of Malaysia have remained separate.

FRESHWATER FISH

Pahang is home to Peninsular Malaysia's longest river, Sungai Pahang. This waterway and its tributaries are teeming with fish such as *ikan jelawat* (Hoven's carp or sultan fish) and *ikan patin* (silver catfish), an oily fish with a fine texture that is highly prized. *Ikan patin* has no scales and is often served Chinese style, steamed with soy sauce or in either a coconut-based or tamarind-flavoured curry. Temerloh, a small town in the middle of the state, is a great place to try these freshwater fish dishes.

GRILLED FISH IN KUANTAN

The dish that the state capital Kuantan is most famous for is *ikan bakar* (fish barbecued over charcoal). The place to sample it are the food stalls in the village of Tanjung Lumpur, across the Kuantan River from the heart of the city. The most famous stall here is Ana Ikan Bakar Petai, which prepares the fish in a spicy sauce with *petai* (stink beans).

Don't Miss

→ **Ayam golek** A whole chicken, marinated in a sauce made with coconut milk and a mix of spices and aromatics, then roasted over an open fire until golden brown.

→ **Ketupat pulut sotong** Squid stuffed with glutinous rice and simmered in a white gravy flavoured with black pepper and spices like clove, star anise and nutmeg.

→ **Gulai tempoyak patin** A catfish curry flavoured with fermented durian and turmeric.

→ **Gulai asam rong** A sour, slightly bitter-tasting fish curry flavoured with the fruits of rubber trees.

→ **Puding diraja** 'Royal pudding', made from bananas, prunes, *urat emas* (golden strands of cooked batter) and custard.

KELANTAN & TERENGGANU

These east-coast states may be staunchly Malay but they also have links with Thailand, imparting a tendency for spiciness and sweetness in the local cuisine, in which fish and coconut features heavily.

RICE & COCONUT

Being relatively cut off from the rest of Peninsular Malaysia, Kelantan has its own distinct Malay culture, which is reflected in its local cuisine. Coconut and rice are common ingredients, as in *nasi ayam percik*: bone-in cuts of chicken marinated in a spicy coconut-milk sauce, slowly grilled over charcoal and eaten with rice.

Nasi dagang, the *nasi lemak* of the east coast, is a breakfast favourite. In Terengganu the dish is made from a mixture of white glutinous rice, steamed in coconut milk and served with fragrant tuna curry, pickled cucumber and carrots. Kelantan's version of *nasi dagang* uses a wild rice that is a light purple colour and a little glutinous.

NASI KERABU

The most famous dish of Kelantan is *nasi kerabu* (literally 'rice salad'). Its origins are in the cooking of Kelantanese Peranakans. *Nasi kerabu* can also be traced to a similar rice dish popular in southern Thailand known as *khao jam* or *khao yum*. The unique Kelantan factor is the blue colour of the *nasi*, the result of cooking the rice with the petals of *bunga telang* (butterfly pea flower). The pale blue rice is accompanied by a salad of finely shredded raw local herbs and vegetables. Also part of this traditional meal is fried breaded fish, a coconut and fish relish, a spicy *sambal* or two and other condiments such as *budu*, a fermented anchovy sauce that is also a Kelantan speciality.

SEAFOOD SNACKS

In Terengganu, the locals have created countless ways to prepare the wonderful fruits of the sea. The deep-fried pastry *epok epok*, a sort of a cross between a samosa and an empanada, is filled with a mix of fish and grated coconut. *Sata* is a local spin on the fish-paste dish *otak otak*, wrapped in cones fashioned out of banana leaves and grilled. The sugar added to *sata* reflects the regional penchant for sweetness, an influence from the states' northern neighbour, Thailand.

Another Terengganu delicacy is *keropok*, made by grinding sea fish into a paste and mixing it with

LAKSAM

Laksam *are broad, flat rice noodles which features in a laksa dish typical to the east coast of the peninsula, but especially popular in Kelantan. Laksam are served with* kuah putih, *a rich, creamy, fishy coconut gravy, topped with finely shredded local herbs and vegetables and a dollop of* sambal *for a spicy kick.*

Below: Pantai Penarik is one of the most beautiful beaches in Terengganu

sago to create a fishy sausage. If the sausage is steamed-cooked it's known as *keropok rebus*, but it is more commonly deep-fried in long thick strips *(keropok lekor)* or in thin slices *(keropok keping)* to make crispy crackers that are served with chilli sauce. The local recipe for the chilli sauce is a little more sweet than spicy and contains a swig of tamarind juice (yet another indication of the Thai influence here).

Don't Miss

➡ **Nasi kerabu** The rice is tinted blue using the petals of a local flower; the salad is made from finely shredded raw herbs and vegetables.

➡ **Laksam** Flat rice noodles served in a mildly spicy and sour coconut-milk-based gravy.

➡ **Nekbat** Syrup-soaked sponges made from rice flour and eggs.

➡ **Keropok lekor** Enjoy these fish crackers hot and crispy fresh out the fryer, with a dip of sweet chilli sauce.

➡ **Nasi ayam percik** Barbecued chicken marinated with spicy coconut gravy and served with rice.

➡ **Sanggang** A sour fish soup made with lemongrass, galangal, chilli and a light tamarind juice.

SARAWAK

Across the South China Sea, on the island of Borneo, Sarawak is home to indigenous tribes including the Melanau, Iban and Bidayuh. Their cuisine is based on what can be fished from the rivers and seas and foraged in the rainforests.

UMAI

Among the joys of travel in Sarawak is the chance to sample the traditional foods of so many different ethnic groups. The Melanau, one of the oldest indigenous tribes in Sarawak, refer to themselves as *a-likou*, meaning 'people of the river'. A traditional Melanau fisherman's lunch is *umai* – thin slices of raw fish marinated with shallots, chilli, salt and tamarind or calamansi juice. *Umai* is often made with *ikan pirang*, a yellow fish with small bones. Spanish mackerel, black pomfret and shad are also used.

SAGO

The Melanau use the processed pith of the sago palm as the main starch component in their meals. Served instead of rice, sago pellets are made with desiccated coconut, sago flour and rice bran. Sago can also be mixed vigorously with hot water to create *linut* (also known as *ambuyat*), a thick, translucent and bland-tasting paste which is pepped up with *sambal*.

Weevils lay eggs in the rotting pith of the sago trunk that develop into fat, wriggly grubs the size of a man's little finger. These sago grubs are virtually pure protein and are considered a delicacy to be eaten boiled in soups or stir-fried with shallots and ginger – a dish known as *siat* or *butod*. For the brave, they can also be chomped raw and still alive!

SARAWAK LAKSA

Tangy, chewy, spicy, crunchy and thoroughly lip-smacking, Sarawak laksa is a supremely satisfying way to begin the day. It's the dish Sarawakians most often crave when they're away from Borneo and shares little more than its name with the laksa dishes popular in Peninsular Malaysia and Singapore.

Sarawak laksa brings a hot, tangy broth – made with a paste of chilli, garlic, shallots, peanuts, galangal, candlenuts and lemongrass – together with *bee hoon* (vermicelli noodles) and an array of tasty toppings with toothsome textures: bean sprouts, omelette strips, chicken slices, shrimp and chopped coriander. Diners squeeze calamansi lime on top and decide how much

TANGY, CHEWY, SPICY, CRUNCHY AND *thoroughly* **LIP-SMACKING**

Right: Sarawak
laksa with prawns

fiery *sambal belacan* they can handle.

Most purveyors of Sarawak laksa are, like *bee hoon*, of Chinese origin, but in the finest Malaysian tradition, this pungent dish brings together a variety of culinary influences, including classic Peranakan ingredients such as *sambal belacan* and coconut milk.

BAMBOO CHICKEN

A perennial favourite among Sarawak's Dayak tribes is bamboo chicken, known as *ayam pansuh* or *manok pansun* in the Iban language and as *syok tanok darum bu-uruk* in Bidayuh. To make it, rice, chicken and spices such as lemongrass, garlic, ginger and chillies are stuffed into a length of bamboo, which is sealed with turmeric leaves. The cylinder is then cooked near (but not too near) an open fire, thereby infusing the dish with the delicate aromas of bamboo and turmeric

and ensuring that the meat emerges deliciously tender. It's aßn easy and delicious meal to cook at a jungle campfire and eat beneath the stars.

KELABIT HIGHLAND INGREDIENTS

Nestled in Sarawak's remote northeastern corner are the mountains and rainforests of the Kelabit Highlands. The area is home to the Kelabits, an Orang Ulu group who number only about 6500, clustered in the dozen or so villages of Bario. This region is famous throughout Malaysia for its rice, whose grains are smaller and more aromatic than lowland varieties, and for its sweeter-than-sweet pineapples, which are free of the pucker-inducing acidity of their coastal cousins. Another of Bario's celebrated local ingredients is its high-iodine salt, which goes perfectly with local game such as deer and wild boar.

Don't Miss

- ➔ **Bamboo chicken** Succulent pieces of chicken marinated with aromatics and spices and steam-cooked inside a length of bamboo.
- ➔ **Siat** These fat stir-fried sago grubs are a protein-rich regional delicacy.
- ➔ **Umai** Slivers of raw fish marinated with shallots, chilli, salt and tamarind or lime juice.
- ➔ **Tuak** Rice wine. Whether home-brewed or served at a pub, Sarawak's traditional

welcome drink packs a heady alcoholic punch.
- ➔ **Sarawak laksa** The breakfast noodle dish gets its protein from a mix of chicken and shrimp. The gravy has a burnt-sienna-coloured base from toasted rice and coconut, and an acid-sweet perkiness from calamansi lime.
- ➔ **Kek lapis** Sarawak is famous all over Malaysia for the intricate and colourful striped layer cakes sold in Kuching's Main Bazaar.

From top: Tun
Sakaran Marine
Park; A resident of
the Borneo jungle;
Celebrating a
Murut festival

SABAH

Covering the northwest corner of Borneo, Sabah is home to some 42 different ethnic groups, each with individual food cultures. All draw on the state's abundant supply of seafood, river fish, deer, wild boar, game, wild plants, herbs and rainforest fruits.

SOUR FLAVOURS

Sabah's main tribal community are the Kadazan-Dusun. Their most famous dish is *hinava tongii*, slices of fresh raw Spanish mackerel mixed with chilli, ginger and shallots and drenched in lime juice. What sets this dish apart from other marinated raw fish dishes is the addition of the grated seed of the *bambangan*, a variety of wild mango native to Borneo. The Kadazan love the tangy zing that's given to their food by the addition of sour fruits such as *bambangan*, limes and *belimbing asam* from the native *Averrhoa bilimbi* tree.

ALTERNATIVE STARCHES

While rice is cultivated across Sabah, it is not necessarily the staple food of Sabahans; in the north, corn and tapioca are preferred. Just as in Sarawak, in many swampy areas of Sabah the wild sago palm flourishes and sago starch forms part of many Sabahan meals. The Muslim Bisaya people use sago starch to make *ambuyat* – it's the equivalent of Sarawak's *linut*. This thick, gluey mixture is twirled around a chopstick and dipped into a condiment. The most popular dips are *binjai*, made from a local sour fruit, and *tempoyak*, made from fermented durian.

FERMENTED FOODS

The Murut are famous for their *jaruk*, chunks of raw wild boar or river fish packed into a bamboo tube together with salt and cooked rice. The bamboo is sealed with leaves and the contents left to ferment for several weeks or even months. It is finally eaten in small portions with rice or tapioca starch. Another fermented dish made by the Kadazan-Dusun people is *bosou*, also called *noonsom* or *tonsom*. Smoked and pulverised *buah keluak* (nuts from the kepayang tree which grows in Borneo's mangrove

KOTA KINABALU'S NIGHT MARKET

KK's Night Market is an unmissable immersion into local culture. It's authentic, bustling, aromatic and noisy. At the southwest end you will find stalls selling everything from belacan to snake beans. Towards the waterfront are the fish stalls: row upon row of bug-eyed bream, tuna, tiger prawns and red snapper. At the northeast end of the market is a huge hawker centre where you can eat your way through every Malay dish in the book.

swamps) are a key ingredient and act as a preservative. Combined with rice, salt and fresh meat or fish, the mixture is then placed into a sealed jar or container for fermentation.

RICE–BASED ALCOHOLIC DRINKS

Nearly all of Sabah's non-Muslim tribes make alcoholic beverages from steamed glutinous rice and dried yeast. *Tapai* (otherwise known as *pengasai*) is typically made from brown rice and is much loved by the Kadazan-Dusun and Murut. It's consumed from communal jars through bamboo straws. *Lihing*, a gold-coloured alcohol made from sticky rice, is believed to be particularly good for post-natal mothers. It's also used in the recipe of a Kadazan favourite, chicken soup with *lihing* and fresh ginger.

SABAH VEGGIE

Sayur manis, also known as 'Sabah veggie', is a local green leafy vegetable, not unlike spinach, that can be found on the menu at any Chinese restaurant worth its salt in Sabah. It's best served fried with garlic or mixed with fermented shrimp paste. The *sayur manis* plant is a perennial and

can grow about 3m (10ft) high. It is harvested year-round, so tends to be very fresh. However, be very sure to eat this green only if it has been cooked: in its raw state it can be deadly poisonous and has been linked to lung failure.

Don't Miss

● **Hinava** Slices of raw fish mixed with bird's eye chillies, grated ginger and sliced shallots, all marinated in lime juice.
● **Tapai** This alcoholic drink made from fermented brown rice is usually served during Kadazan-Dusun celebration and rites.
● **Jaruk** Made from wild boar or fresh river fish that's packed into a bamboo tube together with rice and salt and fermented for several weeks.
● **Beaufort mee** Handmade smoked noodles are cooked in a wok with slices of pork or seafood and plenty of the leafy vegetable *choy sum*. It's a speciality of the town of Beaufort.
● **Pinasakan sada** A traditional Kadazan-Dusun dish of grilled scad (a kind of fish) and *takob akob* (a wild fruit prized for its tangy skin), fresh turmeric and salt.

Right: Lau Pa Sat is one of Singapore's oldest and biggest hawker centres

SINGAPORE

Singaporeans are obsessed with *makan* (food), from talking incessantly about their last meal to feverishly photographing, critiquing and posting about it online. This is hardly surprising – the nation's melting pot of cultures has created one of the world's most diverse, drool-inducing culinary landscapes.

HOW IT ALL BEGAN

Singapore has a history of migration. As each ethnic group and subgroup arrived on the island it brought its own cuisine. Each type of food remains largely undiluted to this day, but as often happens when cultures are transplanted far from home, local variations and customs have crept in. Just as the people of Singapore developed their own characteristics the longer they were separated from their homelands, the character of dishes such as fish-head curry, chilli crab and *yu sheng* (raw fish salad eaten at Chinese New Year) have all evolved from traditional favourites. Singaporeans live to eat, and while you're here you might as well join them.

For Singaporeans, what's on the plate is far more important than the quality of the china (or plastic) it's served on. The smartest-dressed businessman is as comfortable sitting on a cheap plastic chair at a plastic table and wading into a S$4 plastic plate of *char kway teow* as he is eating S$90 crabs in an air-conditioned restaurant. Combine this unpretentiousness with infinite variety, high standards of hygiene and the prevalence of the English language, and you have some of the best and most accessible eating opportunities in Southeast Asia.

FISH-HEAD CURRY

Legend has it that fish-head curry was created by Mariam Jacob Gomez, a Keralan cook at his restaurant on Selegie Rd in the 1940s. Fish heads are not a common ingredient of Indian cuisine, but Gomez suspected that this recipe would appeal to his Chinese diners who considered fish heads a delicacy. The dish was a hit and today you'll find fish-head curry served across both Malaysia and Singapore. Gomez's South Indian original uses coconut milk for a rich and creamy sauce, while Peranakans prepare it with *asam* (tamarind juice) for a lighter, tangier flavour.

YU SHENG

Developed by four Singaporean master chefs in the 1960s, *yu sheng* is a salad of paper-thin raw fish, finely grated vegetables, candied melon and lime, red and white pickled ginger, pomelo sacs, sesame seeds, jellyfish and peanuts tossed in a dressing. It's eaten on the seventh day of the Chinese New Year in the belief that it will bring diners prosperity and good luck. The inspiration for the dish is the Cantonese tradition of consuming raw fish strips during New Year. The chefs added new ingredients and entwined symbolic significance into the dish and its presentation.

CHILLI CRAB

While crab curries do exist within the Indian culinary oeuvre, Singapore chilli crab has a sweet and spicy sauce, thickened with eggs, that is closer to what is considered sweet-and-sour sauce in the West. The creation of the dish, which is available at seafood restaurants across the island, is attributed to the wife of Lim Choon Ngee, a chap who owned a seafood restaurant along the Kalang River. Today, his son Roland keeps the family tradition alive at Roland Restaurant on Marine Parade Central.

Chilli crab is a messy affair; you may as well embrace the messiness involved, dispense with the utensils, and attack the pieces with your fingers just as any self-respecting local would. Be sure to dig into the crevices of crab where the tenderest morsels reside. It is perfectly acceptable to dip this meat into the sauce of the communal platter.

SINGAPORE LAKSA

Singapore laksa is often called Katong laksa after the district of the island with which the noodle dish is most associated. It is also very similar (if not identical!) in its recipe and preparation to Nonya laksa – unsurprisingly so,

Left: Gardens by the Bay botanical garden
Above: Chilli crab

as Katong is a district long settled by Peranakan families. Brothers Ng Juat Swee and Ng Chwee Seng started selling their version of Katong laksa in a coffeeshop on East Coast Rd in 1950. By the late 1990s there were four rival stalls along the same stretch of East Coast Rd, each claiming to sell the original Katong laksa. It's not a hard-and-fast science but experts say a sandy texture to the gravy – provided by the addition of dried prawns – is usually an indication of a Singapore laksa. Other differences are that Nonya laksa is topped with blood cockles and fresh cucumber, while sitting atop a Singapore laksa you'll more typically have a boiled egg and a slice of fish-paste sausage.

CHICKEN RICE

Although almost every country with a history of immigration from China has a version of this recipe, Singapore's chicken rice has risen to iconic status and is considered one of the island's national dishes. The classic recipe is poached breasts of chicken paired with chicken-stock flavoured rice and served with chilli sauce and cucumber slices. It evolved from a chicken-rice dish made by Hainanese immigrants to the island. Restaurants and hawker stalls serving the dish have been around since at least the late 1940s; one of the most famous is Tian Tian Hainanese Chicken Rice at Chinatown's Maxwell Food Court.

However, it was the chef Chan Hon Meng's preparation of the

dish at his stall Liao Fan Soya Sauce Chicken Rice & Noodle
in the Chinatown Complex that caught the attention of
Michelin judges in 2016. The stall was awarded the coveted
star in the first edition of Singapore's *Michelin Guide*.
Quick to build on his success, Chan Hong Meng rebranded
his stall Hawker Chan and set up franchises across
Singapore and internationally. The new shops have a more
McDonald's-esque vibe; stick to the Chinatown Complex
original if you've got time to wait in the snaking queue.

BAK CHOR MEE

The other queue you'll surely want to join is at Hill
Street Tai Hwa Pork Noodle. This second-generation
hawker stall, established in 1932, was also was awarded
a Michelin star. It's a little further out of the way, about
a 10-minute walk from the Lavender MRT station, but
the queue here is shorter (though you can still expect
a lengthy wait, especially at lunchtime). The object of
desire? Teochew-style *bak chor mee:* springy noodles,
tender pork and liver slices, crispy flat fish and a punch-
packing vinegary chilli sauce.

NEW-GENERATION HAWKERS

As the older generation of hawkers begins to retire, a new
breed of innovative incomers are taking up the challenge
of dishing out great meals on the cheap. Food trucks
have not fully taken off in Singapore like they have in
other countries due to the nation's myriad government
regulations, one being that the truck must remain in the
same location. Food truckers have thus begun to set up in
the city's hawker centres. The most notable is Timbre +,
where you'll find old-school hawker stalls jostling up to
Airstream caravans selling everything from fancy French
cuisine to salted egg-yolk chicken wings. Throw in some
shipping containers covered in street art, a craft-beer bar
and night-time live-music acts, and Timbre + is one of the
hippest joints in town to grab a meal.

Don't Miss

⊖ **Durian** Sure, the fruit isn't cultivated on the island, but the experience of digging into the spiky shells alongside locals at tables lining Geylang Rd is a true gastronomic delight not to be missed.

⊖ **Chilli crab** Dig into the scrumptious local speciality with your fingers, then mop up the eggy, thick sauce with French bread or deep-fried *man tou* (plain Chinese buns, a northern Chinese staple).

⊖ **Singapore laksa** The gravy is rich, sour and deep in flavour, and includes deep-fried anchovies, coconut milk and *belacan*. It has an iconic garnish of fish cakes.

⊖ **Fish-head curry** Go on, it tastes fabulous – especially the soft muscle around the eyeballs.

SINGAPORE'S DINING DISTRICTS

COLONIAL DISTRICT, THE QUAYS & MARINA BAY

The handful of restaurants in the National Gallery Singapore brings some top-notch dining options to the Colonial District, while those who have a thing for celeb restaurants will be in their element in Marina Bay Sands. Head to the Quays for an endless choice of breezy waterfront restaurants and bars.

CHINATOWN

Chinatown is the best place to eat in Singapore, hands down. An endless array of choices await – from hawker centres to fine-dining haunts – serving everything from chicken rice to traditional Peranakan dishes, modern Australian to moreish Mexican. There's a great place to eat on almost every street, but you'll find some of the newer spots on Keong Saik Rd.

LITTLE INDIA & KAMPONG GLAM

Little India boasts some of the best cheap eats this side of the subcontinent, though this being Singapore, you don't have to stray far from hawker HQ, aka the Tekka Centre, to find Vietnamese and Italian worth crossing town for. Head to Kampong Glam for a Middle Eastern food fix, or to while away an afternoon in a cute cafe.

ORCHARD ROAD

Mall-heavy Orchard Rd offers many places to satisfy your hunger. Take your pick from high-end culinary heavyweights, international chain restaurants and bustling indoor hawker food courts.

EASTERN SINGAPORE

This area of the island is home to some exceptional food, from the multicultural delights of Joo Chiat (Katong) to the superb seafood along the east coast. Hardier souls might brave the nightly, never-sleeping sleaze of Geylang, where some great food lurks among the sex workers and punters. Look out for durian stalls along the way.

HOLLAND VILLAGE & DEMPSEY HILL

Two expat-heavy districts stacked with chic bistros and leafy garden restaurants, serving predominantly Western food.

NORTHERN & CENTRAL SINGAPORE

In these residential areas it's all about local hawker centres, decades-old bakeries tucked in quaint shophouses and bustling family restaurants on housing estates.

SENTOSA ISLAND

This resort island offers everything from fine-dining hideaways to fish and chips on the beach.

WEST & SOUTHWEST SINGAPORE

Jurong East MRT station is connected to two major malls with fantastic food options, and Kranji MRT station also has cafes and restaurants. Trendy Timbre+ offers traditional and new-age hawker stalls, live music and craft beers.

EAT MALAYSIA & SINGAPORE

Published in May 2022 by Lonely Planet Global Limited
CRN 554153
www.lonelyplanet.com
ISBN 978 18386 9518 7
© Lonely Planet 2022
10 9 8 7 6 5 4 3 2 1
Printed in Malaysia

Written by: Simon Richmond
General Manager, Publishing: Piers Pickard
Publisher: Robin Barton
Editors: Bridget Blair, Polly Thomas
Designer: Jo Dovey
Cover illustration: © Muti, Folio Art
Spot illustrations: Louise Sheeran
Cartographer: Rachel Imeson
Print Production: Nigel Longuet

Lonely Planet Global Limited
Digital Depot, Roe Lane (off Thomas St),
Digital Hub, Dublin 8, D08 TCV4
Ireland

STAY IN TOUCH lonelyplanet.com/contact